Would Like to Meet

About the authors:

Tracey Cox

Tracey Cox is one of the world's foremost writers on sex and relationships as well as a TV presenter. Born in the UK, Tracey spent many years in Australia where she edited *Cosmopolitan* magazine and had a weekly national radio show. She moved to London to host her first television series, *Hot Love* which was followed by *Hotter Sex*. Since then, Tracey has made numerous appearances on television including a regular slot on *Lorraine* (Sky One). Tracey has a degree in psychology and contributes regularly to leading magazines across the globe. Her books *Hot Sex: How to Do It* and *Hot Relationships: How to Have One* are international bestsellers. She is happily settled in Richmond, London.

Jay Hunt

Jay Hunt has worked as a producer in television since 1990. Her credits include *Hotter Sex* (Sky One), *Holiday Favourites* (BBC1), *The Vanessa Show* (BBC1) and *Esther* (BBC2). As a stylist she has worked extensively with numerous television presenters and also as a personal dresser to clients in the UK and the USA.

Jeremy Milnes

Jeremy Milnes is a 44-year-old trained actor, drama teacher and communication, confidence and assertiveness tutor. In between acting jobs and qualifying as a Samaritan Listener he worked as a Learning Mentor in a school in North London. His acting credits include the lead male role in the film *The Vapour Trail* and numerous roles with touring theatre companies. He is currently working towards full qualification as a personal counsellor.

Would Like to Meet

Tracey Cox
Jay Hunt
Jeremy Milnes

This book is published to accompany the television series *Would Like to Meet*, produced by Talkback Productions and first broadcast on BBC2 in 2001.
Series Editor: Daisy Goodwin
Series Producer: Alannah Richardson
For more information on relationships and *Would Like to Meet,* see the website at www.bbc.co.uk/relationships

Published by BBC Worldwide Ltd
Woodlands
80 Wood Lane
London W12 OTT

First published 2002
Copyright © Talkback Productions Ltd 2002
The moral right of Jay Hunt, Tracey Cox and Jeremy Milnes to be identified as the authors of this work has been asserted.

ISBN: 0 563 48843 3

Commissioning Editor: Nicky Copeland
Project Editor: Helena Caldon
Copy Editor: Trish Burgess
Art Director: Sarah Ponder
Design: Grade Design Consultants
Production Controller: Christopher Tinker
Picture Researcher: David Cottingham

Set in Helvetica Neue and OCRB
Printed and bound by in Great Britain by The Bath Press
Cover printed by Bellmont Press, Northampton

BBC Worldwide would like to thank Photonica for permission to reproduce photographs on pp10, 52, 94 and 134, and Mike Hogan for the photograph on p.6

Contents

Introduction

Would Like to Meet is a dating make-over show with a difference. Instead of simply matching two people up, then sitting back, stocking up on confetti and waiting for the wedding, we reckoned it would be a lot more helpful long-term to make people more dateable. We aim to arm them with dating and relationship skills, so if the date doesn't work out, they're not back at square one but ready, willing and able to get back out there and attract loads more potential partners.

That's why our success on *WLTM* doesn't depend on the contributors clasping hands and skipping off into the sunset with their final date. What's more important to us is how they rate the date – and themselves – at the end of the evening. Did they feel confident, sexy, comfortable? Were they happy with how they looked, sounded, felt, performed? Most importantly, even if their date didn't think they were sex-on-legs (or vice versa) are they optimistic others will? Nothing gets our hearts pounding with pride more than taking someone who dreaded the whole dating process ('I just want to find someone special so I don't have to do it any more') to the point where they feel totally relaxed with it ('On second thoughts, maybe I'd like to play the field for a while').

This book takes you through a written version of the six-week process we normally apply in the flesh to our TV contributors. It's based on our 'inside-out formula': getting the outer you to reflect the inner you. First we help you to discover what your clothes, conversation and body language are saying about you. Then we help you to adjust all three so that you're sending out the right signals. Quite frankly, if you can take a good, long, objective look at yourself and conclude that your appearance, image, body language, conversation and manner are all giving out the signals you want, you don't need this book. If you're not convinced that's so, or wouldn't have a clue where to start to find out, stick with us. (The truth is that most people are totally unaware of what all these things say about them.) In the last stage we help you to identify what else might be interfering with your dating desirability, spell out specific and practical techniques designed to fix any problems, pinpoint what's working and what's not – and end up with a happy, glowing, attractive, sexy and oh-so-dateable you at the end of it all!

Jay Hunt, a celebrity stylist, fashion guru and all-round Piercingly Perceptive Person, deals with the externals – the way you look. Don't be lulled into a false sense of security, though: this isn't superficial stuff. Our clothes send a strong message to others, as well as giving clues about what we think of ourselves. (Addicted to black? Could be you're hiding from something.) Prepare to answer some deep, probing questions and face up to yourself in the mirror.

Jeremy Milnes, former drama teacher, counsellor and all-round confidence booster, whips your conversation into shape. As well as working with your words – what you're saying and how you're saying it – he builds internal confidence so that you've got the courage to get out there and try everything out.

I'm a psychologist and spend a great deal of time analyzing and advising about sex, flirting, body language and relationships in general both in books and on television. I focus particularly on body language because the way you walk, stand and sit speaks volumes about you. My job is to correct any off-putting habits or postures, teach you how to read other people's body language (so you know when you're in with a chance) and divulge all the tricks of the trade when it comes to flirting.

While the three of us are all concentrating on different aspects of you, our common goal is always the same: to make you look, feel, act and be the best you can be. This doesn't, by the way, mean we're lookist or ageist. It's not about 'dumbing down' or pandering to the 'hide your brain under batting eyelashes' philosophy (stupid is definitely not sexy). It's not about over-generalizing either. We're all – thankfully – far too individual to reduce everything and everyone down to one common formula. It is about reducing the risk of rejection from potential dates, and that's something we're not apologizing for.

There's also a definite emphasis on 'packaging'. We're not for a second insinuating that what's underneath isn't important: it is. Our personalities account for about 70 per cent of what someone falls in love with. But it's the other 30 per cent that initially attracts people and makes them want to meet us and find out more. The cruel truth is that people make up their minds whether they fancy you or not within four minutes, sometimes as little as a minute and a half. Given the statistics, we believe it pays to work on clothes, image, body language and initial conversation to at least get you to first base. After all, most of us are fine once we're chatting: it's the initial bit that stumps us. But never again!

This book isn't just instructional, it's fun. It includes lots of lists and information boxes, so you can dip in and out whenever the mood strikes and always find something snappy and relevant. We've skipped the long, touchy-feely lectures about life, love and the universe, and vague (not to mention useless) advice like 'be yourself and others will like you' for more realistic hints and tips. Some of them cut rather close to the bone, but that's what we're here for, right? We're the bossy best friend who isn't afraid to tell you things as they are because we really do have your best interests at heart.

While *WLTM* is fun and all about getting out there and strutting your stuff, you need to shed more than just your wardrobe to get results. You've also got to shake off all those not-so-fab beliefs about yourself that you've picked up from exes, family or friends (however well-intentioned they might have been). In order to become the person you want to be, you have to know who that is, which is a tall order. It requires a fair bit of soul-searching and facing up to some (sometimes unpleasant) home truths. We can hold your hand via the book but it helps immeasurably if you've got a good friend doing it in real life as well.

Don't kid yourself: it's not an easy process. But it is worth it. While none of us can promise this book will guarantee you finding the perfect partner, we can promise we'll do a great job of getting you to the point where you're having so much fun flirting with Mr or Ms Maybe you won't really care.
Want to give it a whirl? Then start reading...

Tracey Cox
London, June 2002

PS: All of us make 'girl' and 'boy' references. We know you're not 13 any more, but honestly, 'woman' and 'man' sound like something your mum and dad would say, while 'male' and 'female' scream science teacher. We'd also like to apologize to our gay readers for not referring to boy/boy and girl/girl combinations – it all gets too confusing. Nonetheless, this book really is for everyone, regardless of age or sexuality.

1

Body Language and Flirting

Tracey Cox

You're on a blind date, waiting for the mystery person to arrive – fiddling with the cutlery, fiddling with your clothes, cursing whoever set you up and generally thinking 'How did I get talked into this?' Then, from the corner of your eye, you see the back of a person's head, watch them ask the waiter something and then, oh my god, they're pointing at your table! Which means this must be the person who Sarah/Gloria/Paul/Harry said was just soooo perfect for you, you had to meet! Your heart beats even faster, you hold your breath and then they start walking towards you. In less than the 30 seconds it takes for them to walk from door to table, you'll have already decided your match-making friend either deserves to be godparent to the many children the two of you will obviously create, or deserves a bullet straight between the eyes.

In other words, an astonishing 80 per cent of you will already have decided what you think of this person by the time they reach your side. How? Almost every facet of our personality is evident from our appearance, posture, the way we move and hold ourselves. We make outrageous snap judgements about someone's class, wealth, intelligence, occupation, success level and sexiness based purely on appearance and body language. But it's with good reason because bodies speak louder than words. First impressions are hard to shake because they're usually accurate. It doesn't matter if your blind date's first sentence is, 'Hi. The name's Bond. James/Jane Bond.' If they've slunk their way over to you, with shoulders drooped, eyes lowered and less energy than a holiday rep the morning after the tour before, suave and sophisticated aren't going to be the words that spring to mind.

At this point you'd be forgiven for asking, 'What's the point of this body language stuff if it's all set in stone?' Well, I'm a strong believer in the fake-it-till-you-make-it theory. If your body language reflects your personality, then it's logical to assume particular gestures and behaviours are associated with particular personalities and images. This means that if you know what these things are, and imitate or adopt all the body language gestures of the person you want to be, you'll be seen as that person. Right? You bet it's right!

Think about it. It's a Catch-22 situation, one that is totally biased in your favour. Change the way you appear to people by altering your body language and you change the way people see you. This, of course, affects the way they react to you, which has the spin-off of changing the way you react back to them. And so the chain reaction continues: you start behaving as if you are the person they think you are because that's the way they're treating you, because that's the way you appear. (Phew!) In the initial stages, you're faking it – pretending with your body language to be something that you are not (sexy/confident). But by the end of the exercise, the body language reflects the real you because you've become that person. Other people's response to you faking sexiness/confidence has given you the courage and feedback to become sexy/confident in reality. It doesn't matter how you feel on the inside, you can give the illusion of being whoever you want on the outside simply by getting your body language right. (Get it wrong and the opposite happens.)

Interesting fact number one: Body language isn't a fad – it's as old as the human race.

Interesting fact number two: Body language has never been handier or more applicable than in today's society.

Like it or not, we live in a world where decisions are made fast. Speed-dating (meeting, and usually dismissing, potential dates within a few minutes or less) might be the latest dating technique, but in reality we've all been speed-dating for years. Here one minute, gone the next nanosecond: we whizz in and out of each other's lives faster than you can say 'Can't talk – got a deadline to meet'. As the saying goes, you've only got one chance to make a good first impression – and the quickest way to do so is through body language.

If you're still not remotely seduced by the science of body language after all this talk, chances are you're stuck on the it's-all-about-having-your-arms-crossed myth. Truth is, that's never been the case because you can't ever judge on one body language gesture alone. Sitting with your arms crossed can mean you're protecting yourself emotionally and shutting out the other person. But it's just as likely to mean you're freezing cold, having a fat day, covering the coffee stain from the accident you had on the tube, or that's just the way you sit. That's why most body language experts suggest you look for clusters of behaviour – usually at least four body language signs – rather than try to read someone on one thing alone. That's the first thing you learn: look at the whole picture. Use common sense. Body language is a great indicator of how someone's feeling, but often it's the change in someone's body language that is most telling. If your date moves from leaning forward, arms open and resting on their legs, smiling and looking lovingly into your eyes to suddenly sitting back, arms folded, lips pursed and brow crinkled, you don't need to be a body language expert to guess something's changed the mood and upset them. It's all about context.

Quite frankly, I'm the first to admit that this isn't an infallible science. But I'll tell you something else: there's a lot more evidence to support the theory of body language than you think, and it's fascinating to watch and study, not to mention effective to the point of performing miracles of the walk-on-water variety. I've seen people's lives alter instantly, simply by getting them to change one small, seemingly insignificant thing – like standing up straight and looking the world in the eye. Nothing will bond you more effectively to another human being than leaning forward, touching them and doing what's called 'mirroring'. In fact, understanding the messages your body is sending others, and being able to read the messages others are sending you, is one of the most useful dating skills you'll ever learn.

Now I've got you nicely paranoid it seems like a good time to find out what you're like in the dating stakes. Fill in the questionnaire that follows, then let's get started...

Rate your own date

Take a test and find out how you score on the *WLTM* flirt scale.

1. My relationship history has been:

a. Boringly average: I've had a few serious, long-term relationships and a smattering of one-night stands.

b. Pathetic by most people's standards: I've been in love once or twice but am rarely pro-active and have little experience in dating or relationships.

c. Rich in quantity, if not quality. My problem's not getting a date, it's finding someone I want to settle down with.

2. If there's a room full of people, you can be guaranteed I'll choose:

a. The person most likely to break my heart.

b. The best-looking/sexiest person in the room.

c. The safe bet: the girl/guy you'll take home to Mum, but won't necessarily be proud to parade in front of your friends.

3. When I walk into a room, I tend to:

a. Walk tall and proud, pause at the entrance to scan and see who's there, then head for the most interesting group/person.

b. Look down, move fast and hope like hell no one notices me. Once in there, I'll do a great job of blending with the furniture.

c. Scan the room for someone I know and scuttle to their side, then (after a few drinks) venture forth and start chatting to friendly-looking strangers.

4. Flirting is:

a. A necessary evil: you have to do it to get someone's attention but I'm sooooo relieved when we're officially a couple and the game-playing is over.

b. The most fun I'll ever have standing up.

c. Something I could never carry off in a billion years. Even if someone flirted with me, which is highly unlikely, I wouldn't know how to respond, so would blow it anyway.

5. I'm one of those people who:

a. Wait until I'm happy with my appearance before I leave home, but still keep an eye on things when I'm out by smoothing out the creases and checking everything is how it should be.

b. Constantly fiddle with my clothes. If I feel tense or stressed, I often tug at my collar, undo buttons, play with cuffs or whatever else I can fiddle with.

c. Don't really think about how I look. I'm more the type to pull on clean clothes and then forget about them. Rather than fiddle with my clothes, I'll stand still.

6. I see someone I fancy across a crowded room. I'd probably try and get their attention by:

a. Hoping they notice me and come over. No way am I confident enough to approach them.

b. Glancing over to see if they're ever looking my way. Maybe if I catch their eye and we're both checking each other out and have a smile, I'll make a move.

c. Making eye contact, smiling, then walking over to talk to them.

7. I'm definitely interested in them but not so sure the feeling is reciprocated. I'll try to find out by:

a. Making semi-serious flirtatious jokes about us fancying each other/seeing each other again and seeing what response I get. If it's favourable, I might get up the courage to suggest a date.

b. Leaning forward, touching them, whispering naughty suggestions into their ear.

c. Seeing if they stay talking to me or suggest another meeting. If they ask to see me again, I assume they're interested.

8. Touchy-feely people are:

a. Sexy. I'm very comfortable with touch and I like people who aren't unnerved when I touch them.

b. OK in the right circumstances. If the timing's right, if it's someone I quite like and they're not too over the top, it can be quite nice.

c. Highly embarrassing and to be avoided at all costs.

9. Mr or Ms Perfect will probably turn up:

a. When I'm ready to settle down.

b. When I least expect it. I just hope I manage to be in the place I'm supposed to be when they do.

c. I'm not sure I believe in Mr or Ms Perfect any more, but I'm pretty confident I'll know a good thing when I see it.

10. I'm quite good at reading other people's body language:

a. Are you mad? I wouldn't know where to start.

b. I'm probably OK – I haven't really tested it but I sort of know if someone fancies me or not. If anything, it's lack of confidence that stops me taking it further.

c. I'm pretty confident in deciding who's single, who's interested, who's married, who's not open to invitations, just by watching. Most people give themselves away through eye contact.

11. The best way to flirt with someone on a first date is to:

a. Be on your best behaviour.

b. Show more flesh – undo a few buttons to reveal cleavage or a muscled chest.

c. Be attentive, act interested and pay them loads of compliments.

12. I'm with a group of friends and eager to impress one person. Which is sexier?:

a. To impress the group, even if it does mean rattling on a bit over-enthusiastically about my latest project to the point where I knock over the wine.

b. To sit quietly and gaze at them adoringly.

c. To make sure they know I'm watching them, then focus so intently on their eyes and best body bits that they're unnerved and wonderfully vulnerable to any compliments or moves I might make.

13. My first dates usually finish with me:

a. Cooking breakfast the next day.

b. Wondering if they're thinking the same thing I am – and wondering if they've drunk as much as I have.

c. Lying in bed alone, worrying if they had a good time or not.

14. If I go out with a group of friends, I'm usually:

a. The person most likely to be stuck with the non-fanciable but perfectly nice person you try really hard to ditch but never succeed in doing so out of politeness.

b. The person left alone, propping up the bar or dashing out the door at the first available opportunity.

c. The first to be approached or make the approach/be chatted up or do the chatting up.

15. Someone I'm not interested in has made a beeline for me. I react by:

a. Chatting politely while surreptitiously sending 'Save me!' signals to a friend.

b. I'm too busy chatting up someone I do fancy to notice.

c. Being grateful. Few people approach me, and who knows – they might grow on me.

16. I'm noticing the person I'm with seems to be doing whatever I am and mirroring my movements. This is:

a. Very good – it means they're interested.

b. Making me feel a bit weird. Are they making fun of me by imitating me?

c. Good – I think. It's oddly comforting, even if I don't really know what's going on. It makes me think they're on my level.

17. If someone is attracted to me, they're likely to lean toward me. True or false?

a. Wouldn't have a clue. You're not talking my language.

b. It seems logical.

c. Of course. If you want to get close to someone, that's what you do.

18. I'm pushing through a crowded bar on the way to the loo. I catch the eye of someone I'm interested in and they smile. On the way back, I'm not so sure they're keen because they're talking to someone else and don't even look up when I pass. I now assume:

a. I imagined it in the first place.

b. They're chatting to their long-lost cousin and they'll soon come to their senses and seek me out.

c. They were interested but got a better offer.

19. The person I'm chatting up keeps looking at my mouth. This probably means:

a. They've noticed I've got really bad teeth.

b. I've got spinach caught between my teeth.

c. They're imagining what it's like to kiss me.

20. I'm dumped after three dates. I quite liked the person, even if they weren't the love of my life. I react by:

a. Ringing up girl/boyfriend number two, three or four. See! It pays to have a few in reserve.

b. Feeling a little thrown, but as long as I can look back and see the signals it was about to happen, I'm OK about it.

c. Devastated. These were the first dates I've had in years and I was counting on this person being The One.

ADD UP YOUR SCORE

1.	a. 2	b. 1	c. 3
2.	a. 1	b. 3	c. 2
3.	a. 3	b. 1	c. 2
4.	a. 2	b. 3	c. 1
5.	a. 3	b. 2	c. 1
6.	a. 1	b. 2	c. 3
7.	a. 2	b. 3	c. 1
8.	a. 3	b. 2	c. 1
9.	a. 3	b. 1	c. 2
10.	a. 1	b. 2	c. 3
11.	a. 1	b. 3	c. 2
12.	a. 2	b. 1	c. 3
13.	a. 3	b. 2	c. 1
14.	a. 2	b. 1	c. 3
15.	a. 2	b. 3	c. 1
16.	a. 3	b. 1	c. 2
17.	a. 1	b. 2	c. 3
18.	a. 1	b. 3	c. 2
19.	a. 1	b. 2.	c. 3
20.	a. 3	b. 2	c. 1

If you scored 20–30...

You don't just wish the floor would open up and swallow you, it has! You walk like you're melting into the pavement and slink through the dating scene like a frightened animal, sticking to the shadows and only emerging if someone makes the effort to coax you out of there. Your natural dating style is to do nothing but hang around hopefully in case someone else has the courage to do something about the two of you getting together. Always ready to believe the negative, you haven't a clue where to start with flirtatious body language, and even if you could read theirs, I doubt you'd believe someone was interested in you unless they banged you on the head, caveman style. Read this entire book cover to cover, then go back to the beginning and work your way through slowly and seriously, but this time believe in it – and yourself.

If you scored 31–50...

All right, you're sort of there. You scored pretty well on both dating attitude and the body language barometer: the only thing between you and relationship nirvana is confidence. Taking a wild guess, I'd say you've just come out of a nice, comfy, long-term relationship that has gone horribly (if predictably) wrong and thrown your confidence. You did OK on the singles scene before meeting Ms/Mr Thought-You-Were-The-One but feel a bit nervous about meeting Ms/Mr Are-You-Certain-You're-It-And-Not-Going-To-Hurt-Me-Again. The flirting/body language skills are in place, along with a nice dollop of sensitivity, realism and good old-fashioned romanticism. A rather large injection of courage wouldn't go astray though.

If you scored 51–60...

Quite frankly, you're so adept at the flirting/dating game, I'm surprised you've even picked up this book, let alone taken time out from your busy social schedule to do the quiz – which speaks volumes in itself. I mean, let's face it: you know most of the obvious moves and understand the basic psychology behind them. So unless you're flicking through this book while sitting in a dentist's waiting room, something's obviously wrong. Could it be you've reduced the whole flirting game/dating/lust/life to a predictable formula and have the whole thing so under control that you don't get any kicks any more? If it's a problem of quality rather than quantity, you need to concentrate more on being aware of the signals you're sending than picking up on those sent to you. Oh, and you might want to do something about mending that broken heart. Your behaviour screams of being super-successful in replacing the empty space in your bed; not so the hole in your heart/head.

I hope this questionnaire has given you a better idea of your personal flirting style and focused you a little on your attitude to life, love and relationships. Armed with that essential info, let's get to work.

Bodies speak louder than words

Under pressure, our bodies leak – and I don't just mean perspiration. They leak information about our true feelings. Pretend all you like that you're having a wonderful time at Aunt Mary's 60th birthday party ('Of course I wouldn't rather be down the pub with my mates. I know the football's on, but I'd much rather be here with you. Honest!'), but your feet will still draw circles in the air, the fingers of one hand drum a hole in the arm of the sofa and the other hand prop up your head – all classic signs of boredom.

Other indicators include pursed lips, shoulders so tense they're around our ears, shallow breathing, biting our lips, picking our cuticles, touching our mouths... All the gestures our body makes tell a story.

A lot of the time we're unaware of the signals our bodies are sending others. We're not the only ones: the person receiving the signals usually hasn't got a clue what their subconscious is processing to give them the conclusion they're reaching (this person likes/doesn't like me/is bored/having a good time). Asked to pinpoint how they knew they'd overstepped the mark with that story about their ex, and they're likely to say 'instinctually'. It's unlikely they'll say 'Because you leant away from me and put one arm across your body in a partial arm block.' The fact is that it doesn't really matter if they know why. The end result is still the same: your body language is largely responsible for the impression someone has of you.

THE SEVEN DEADLY BODY LANGUAGE SINS

Given the power of the secret messages we send out, it's worth taking a look through the following checklist to make sure you're not guilty of any sins. Most of us chalk up one or two sins in certain situations, but if your score is five and over, best get yourself a big cup of coffee (or a very stiff drink). You're not going anywhere until you've committed the following to memory – and done your homework.

SIN 1:   ## MELTING INTO THE PAVEMENT

What it says about you: If you don't think much of yourself, chances are you slink your way through life, keeping a low profile – literally. People with low self-esteem try to blend with the pavement: they slump their shoulders, bow their heads and generally make themselves look as small as possible. When forced to stand still, it's quite obvious they're wishing the floor would open up and swallow them – their whole body is pointing towards it.

Fix it by: Simply standing up nice and straight, just like good old Mum told you to. If you think highly of yourself, you hold yourself high. It's that simple. People associate an erect posture with self-assured, dominant personalities. You do, too, which is why it's possible to trick yourself into thinking you're far more competent and capable than you really are if you pull those shoulders back and stand tall.

Instant result: You'll appear and feel more confident.

SIN 2:   ## LOOKING AT THE FLOOR

What it says about you: Avoid looking at people and you avoid connecting with them. The real reason you're gazing downward is probably because you're shy – the kindest interpretation people will make of this gesture. Others will think you're not interested in them or anything they're saying (if you can't even be bothered raising your eyes to fake interest, what hope have they got?), arrogant (it's rude not to look at someone who is talking to you), or nervous and slightly dodgy in character (avoid looking someone in the eye and they automatically assume you're hiding something).

Fix it by: Lifting your eyes. If you're too shy to make direct eye contact, at least look straight ahead rather than downward. Or shift your gaze so you're looking just above the other person's head or slightly to the side. True, people will start to feel weirdly self-conscious (and worry that their hair's sticking up or a bit of crisp is stuck to their cheek), but it's better than not connecting with you at all. Once you're used to looking upward, work on meeting people's eyes briefly as you're walking past. Ideally, you'll get to the stage where you can make eye contact while stationary, and comfortably maintain it for periods at a time.

Instant result: If you rectify sins one and two simultaneously you will see remarkable changes in your life. According to communications specialist Gordon Wainwright, simply by making these alterations – walking tall, keeping your shoulders back and looking straight ahead – you'll feel more positive and confident, walk faster, feel fitter, notice more (and react more quickly to) what's happening around you, and think faster and more clearly as well. If that's not enough incentive for you, people will respond differently to you as well. They will agree more with what you say and generally be friendlier. One *WLTM* spectacular success story was Simon, a gorgeous but shy art student from Hull. Simon's self-confidence was at rock-bottom and his body reflected this. Not only wouldn't he meet anyone's eyes, he'd perfected the classic 'If I slump down low enough maybe people won't even notice I'm here' stance. Simply getting him to make eye contact and stand up straight significantly helped to transform him from Mr Uncomfortable to Sex God. Yes, it's that powerful!

SIN 3:   FIDDLING WITH YOUR COLLAR OR SCRATCHING YOUR NECK

What it says about you: If you're constantly scratching your neck or pulling your collar away from it, you might as well have a neon sign hanging round it that reads 'My name's John/Jane and you're making me feel horribly insecure and/or as nervous as hell'. Both gestures are signs of doubt and uncertainty. Interestingly, most of us use the same finger (the index) to scratch, and aim for the same place (just below the ear on the side of the neck). Even more bizarre, almost everyone scratches exactly five times.

People pull their clothes away from their necks when they're in a 'hot spot', literal or otherwise. If you're feeling exposed or caught out, you start sweating, so you pull the clothes away from your neck to get a bit more air. We also do it when we fib. Zoologist and body language expert Desmond Morris found that when we tell a lie, we get a tingling sensation in the face and neck. This is because the heart beats faster when nervous (which most people are when fibbing), the blood pumps harder and the blood vessels dilate. As the skin on the face and neck is particularly sensitive, it's uncomfortable to have clothes rub against it, so we pull them away.

Fix it by: Being aware of what your hands are doing at any given moment (always a good idea). If you feel them hovering anywhere near your neck (and you're not a girl about to launch into a touch-and-tease moment, see page 40), mentally slap yourself and take a quick detour. Turn the movement into a preening (I'm interested in looking good for you) gesture, by smoothing your hair or collar/top.

Instant result: You'll appear more in control, more sincere and more comfortable in any given situation.

SIN 4:   PROPPING UP YOUR FACE WITH YOUR HAND

What it says about you: Putting your hand on the side of your face and leaning on it sends three clear messages:

1. I'm so bored and tired, I can hardly hold my head up.

2. I'm feeling faintly superior and quite possibly judging you while I'm at it. (There's no way we'd sit like that in front of a boss or someone we respected.)
3. I don't like my face much, which is why I'm hiding half of it. (There is one exception to this rule: people sometimes wrap both hands around their face, lean forward and gaze transfixed as if totally besotted with someone. But even if this is your excuse, are you sure you want them to know about it at this early stage?)

Fix it by: Er, removing your hand? That's a great start. Then how about you do something else with it, like run your fingers through your hair and actually hold your hair back from your face? This says, 'Have a good look. I like how I look, so you should too.' Keeping one hand stationary in one position is also restrictive. Not only does it stop you moving your face around (to show it off at different angles), it immediately rules out any chance of touching. (You try hugging with one arm, or leaning across the table to hold someone's hand while keeping your other hand firmly plonked under your chin.)

Instant result: They stop thinking 'I'm boring you/You'd rather be at home tucked up in bed (alone)/I'm talking complete rubbish/Not good enough for you, etc.' Instead, you (and they) are in with a chance. They'll also feel less self-conscious. The other problem with leaning on your hand and gazing at someone is that they feel like they're under a spotlight. Your focus is too intense. Remove your hand, look away as well as at them and they get the space they need. You don't just appear more interested, alive and involved in the conversation, you lighten the mood as well.

SIN 5: LETTING IT ALL HANG OUT

What it says about you: The only thing worse than being tense, rigid and uptight is being so relaxed that you're practically in a sprawled-in-front-of-the-telly pose. Unless you're an ex-Spice girl (more specifically, Posh or Geri), or Calvin Klein's latest male model, none of us can afford to totally relax our tummies. It's unlikely the rest of your body's good enough to relax either. One of *WLTM*'s most famous contributors, George, let it all hang out in a spectacular way on his dummy date. George lived at home with his Greek mum who loved cooking for him almost as much as he enjoyed eating the results. His appetite for life was immensely attractive, but it was a bit of a nightmare for his waistline. When George relaxed his body posture, it wasn't a good look.

Fix it by: Imagining you're about to have sex with Posh/Geri/George Clooney/Brad Pitt/whoever takes your fancy. It's amazing how the thought of being seen naked by someone delicious suddenly makes us pull in our tummies, clench our buttocks, square our shoulders and generally position our bodies in a flattering way.

Instant result: You'll transform yourself from Person I'd Most Like to Watch Telly With to Person Most Likely to Tempt Me to Turn off the Telly (and start having some fun in the process).

SIN 6:

TURNING AWAY FROM THE PERSON YOU FANCY

What it says about you: If we really, really like someone – friend, prospective lover or someone we're already sharing the sheets and remote control with – we give them full body attention and do a complete, 100 per cent body pivot to face them when they're in close proximity. If we're not that fussed, feel intimidated or nervous about the consequences of totally committing our attention, our body language reflects our mood: we'll make a half-hearted turn in the other person's direction, but remain pointing elsewhere with our legs, arms, eyes, chin. Debbie (a *WLTM* contributor notorious for her 'poodle hair'), was sooooooo uninterested in her dummy date that she practically fell asleep. She was a classic example of someone showing lack of interest through body language. Throughout the entire date, Debbie's body language remained stoically facing straight ahead, rather than turned towards her date Sergio. Along with the yawns and eye-rolling the message was pretty clear: I'd rather be at home cleaning the loo than sitting here with you.

Fix it by: Stop to think about the significance of friends, family and prospective dates next time you see them. Pause for a second, then adjust your body to the angle that best represents the level of interest you want them to think they inspire. If you're not so keen, stick with the half-turn. If you're mad about them but they're not getting the hint, do a full body pivot when they say 'Hi' and tap you on the shoulder. I wouldn't take it as far as Linda Blair in *The Exorcist* and madly swivel on the spot, but this will certainly let them know your head's in a spin when they're around. Add a dazzling smile and they can't help but be impressed.

Instant improvement: A 100 per cent body pivot makes people feel very, very noticed and very, very special – both highly desirable if you fancy them. This is even better if it's reciprocated.

SIN 7:

LEANING AWAY FROM SOMEONE WE LIKE

What it says about you: Our posture reflects how much we like the person we're with. Put simply, we lean towards people we like and lean away from people we don't. This is even more pronounced if we're sitting. Watch two close friends perched on bar stools or huddled in a corner having a drink and they're nearly always leaning towards each other, creating a cosy little vacuum-for-two. If you're not convinced it makes one iota of difference, experiment and see for yourself. The next time you talk to a good friend, lean towards them. Chances are they'll behave as normal – talk lots, smile lots – because this is how you naturally behave towards people you like. Now, deliberately lean back from them, keeping everything else constant. See how they talk less, start to look uncomfortable, ask if you're OK, if they're boring you… (At this point, confess that it's a body language experiment, not a power play.)

Fix it by: Apart from mirroring (see page 45), leaning forward with your upper body is the single, most effective I-like-you message you can send someone. Even a child can learn this one: lean forward if you want to get closer physically, emotionally or intellectually); lean back if you don't.

Instant result: Not only will you send 'I'm interested' signals to people you're interested in, this is also a good ploy for looking part of a group if you're feeling ostracized or on the fringes. Watch people in a group and you can tell who's 'in' and who's 'out' by the angle of their bodies. Outsiders typically stand with their weight on one foot/hip, leaning away from the group. Those who are 'in' lean forward with head tipped forward too.

LOOK AND LEARN

OK, so now you know what not to do to spoil your chances of making a good impression, we can move on to the positive stuff. Just one quick word before we do though: you're not the only one who's giving away any negatives in your personality. The person you are dating is too, so it pays to keep your eyes open – especially if you are particularly fond of saying, 'But they were just perfect in the beginning! How was I supposed to know they'd turn out to be a cheat/heartbreaker/addicted to drugs/drink/darts/daytime telly?'

The 'trouble' signs usually start appearing round about date three, when the best behaviour mask starts to slip and the real person emerges from underneath. You hear yourself saying to them, 'Gosh! That's interesting. I've never thought of having a neat Scotch with my morning coffee but hey, why not! Nothing ventured and all that…' and the alarm bells aren't just ringing, they're waking the dead, but you haven't had a date for soooooo long that you can't possibly give up this soon. People look good at the start of relationships because we want them to look good. And please, feel free to continue kidding yourself if you don't mind picking yourself up off the floor when it does all fall apart.

Not so convinced it's fun down there? Well, how about playing it differently next time?

Now, the romantic part of you is going to baulk at this suggestion, but your logical side will certainly agree it's a sensible thing to do. Next time you meet someone new, keep 30 per cent of your heart back for the first three months. Allow 70 per cent of you to let go and enjoy the lovey-dovey, holding-hands-on-the-high-street-smug-couple stuff, but keep the other 30 per cent looking on, like a protective best friend, objectively and mentally running through a checklist to make sure this person is all they seem. Are they treating you well? As an equal? Are they honest? Trustworthy? No one likes getting hurt, and one way to protect your heart is to be careful who you give it to. If you aren't sure of your judgement, ask a trusted friend to meet new dates very early on and give you their honest opinion before your heart (or other bits) get too involved to take good advice.

While you've got your head working overtime to suss them out, take a good, long look at their body language. How their body behaves when put on the spot will be by far your best clue to their sincerity. A smooth talker might wangle their way out of a dodgy situation, but his/her body language never lies. Take note of the following:

HOW TO TELL AN INSINCERE SMILE

It doesn't quite reach their eyes. Put your hand over your mouth, look in the mirror and smile (think about the bar of chocolate you're planning to devour later). See how your eyes sparkle and the skin around them crinkles up? Now do the same exercise with a fake smile (pretending you would really prefer an apple) and see how your eyes barely register the smile or alter in appearance. This is the difference you're watching for.

It's asymmetrical. False smiles aren't even. Usually they're one-sided, look exaggerated and stay fixed in one position for too long. The bottom lip moves less than the top lip. When we smile genuinely or laugh, both lips get involved in the action. When we fake it, we pull the corners of our mouths out and the lips, reluctantly, follow. The bottom lip is longer, so it has less distance to stretch.

HOW TO TELL IF SOMEONE IS LYING

They avoid eye contact. It takes exceptional skill to look someone straight in the eye and lie convincingly. Whether it's because we really do believe the 'windows to the soul' bit or seeing the trust/pain/bewilderment/hope written all over the other person's face is just too much, isn't quite clear. What is clear, though, is that people will try to avoid eye contact with the person they're trying to deceive at all costs. This is where the expression 'shifty eyes' originates from (and why the line 'Look me straight in the eye and tell me it's not true' is used so often in soaps).

He's rubbing an eye and looking up or she's rubbing underneath her eye and looking down. Thank body language expert Allan Pease for this little gem of information: if a man tells a whopper, he'll tend to rub a closed eye vigorously while looking at the floor. Women tend to massage the skin under an open eye and look at the ceiling. (It's spot on, too. Practically foolproof!)

They're hiding their palms. Think of someone begging you to forgive them. The most common gesture they'll use is to hold their hands out in front of them, palms up, towards you. This is where the expression 'showing your hand' (being honest) comes from. Most people find it incredibly difficult to lie with their hands on display, palms up. That's why most of us put them behind our backs, in our pockets, or cross our arms to hide them if we're trying to get away with something. If your new partner does this when asked to clarify something suspicious, be suspicious!

Their hands keep touching their face. Think about it: what do kids do when they tell you something they shouldn't? They immediately clap their hands over their mouth in an attempt to shove the words back in (or, at the very least, stop more coming out). Once we're all grown up, we realize the slapping-hands-across-mouth gesture is a bit of a give-away. But, alas, it's too late. The mouth-covering gesture is learnt, and all we can do at the last moment is divert our hands. That's why we end up touching our nose, scratching our face or half covering our mouth by lightly resting a finger on our top lip while pretending it just feels comfortable to rest it there. Yeah, right. If someone does that to you, by the way, they've either just said something deceitful, or are literally 'zipping their lips' and trying desperately not to blurt out something they shouldn't.

IT'S YOU WHO'VE BEEN CAUGHT OUT IF...

The person you're talking to is yawning, coughing, rubbing an ear or sliding their hands across them, or rubbing their eyes. Think the Three Monkeys: hear no evil, see no evil, speak no evil. When we hear someone tell a lie, we'll often subconsciously cover our ears, so if you're the one doing the talking, you've been caught out. Ditto if the other person covers their mouth – they can't believe what's coming out of yours. If we see something that doesn't ring true, we'll often rub our eyes, as if to check we're not dreaming. All these gestures are subconscious reactions to not believing our eyes or ears.

HOMEWORK:

WATCHING AND BEING WATCHED

For the next two days:

Think about your body and how it's reacting to life. Start noticing how much it responds to your emotions. Feeling a bit down? Don't be surprised if your shoulders slump and you cup your chin in your hand (an 'I need support and there's no one else here, so I might as well support myself' gesture). Feeling happy? You're likely to walk taller, look people straight in the eye, smile. Just spotted someone you've had your eye on for ages? Don't be surprised if you do a typical preening gesture of smoothing your hair (even if you don't have any, old habits die hard). Monitor exactly how your body responds to different emotions and situations and you'll be more aware – ultimately in control of – the messages you're sending.

For the next week:

Be on body alert by staying body aware. How would you look as a sculpture if I were to freeze you at this exact moment? Imagine crowds of people traipsing past your likeness at a world-famous art gallery. (Even worse, your name's on the plaque, so everyone knows that pot-belly belongs to you.) Don't you wish you'd arranged yourself a little better? Sucked in your tummy, flexed that bicep, squared those shoulders? For one week, I want you to pretend this could happen in reality at any given moment. Be acutely conscious of your body and what it's doing at all times. No, I'm not trying to encourage an eating disorder, more a healthy awareness of 'How am I looking?/What signals am I sending?/Am I arranged attractively so I'm shown at my most flattering?' I know, terribly un-PC, but oh-so-effective at making you someone of interest.

Your philosophy:

Assume everyone is watching. Pretend no one is.

Flirting

Some people seem to think flirting is a dirty word – that it means leading people on, playing 'games'. I think that's carrying the whole politically correct business a little too far, don't you? Flirting isn't about making people feel bad – quite the opposite! Flirting is about making people feel good. It operates on the basic smile-and-the-world-smiles-with-you principle.

Flirting simply means relating to others and allowing them to relate to you. It's fun! Flirting is all about being lighthearted, playful, cheeky, adventurous and, most of all, friendly. The main aim of flirting is to make someone feel special. Now, how can that possibly be a bad thing?

Flirting doesn't mean you're out to pull someone. It doesn't mean you're available either. A good flirt isn't desperate, aggressive or in the slightest bit offensive. Sure, if you're flirting with a stranger and you happen to be single and you find them attractive and interesting and would like to get to know them better, you're naturally hoping all the aforementioned will be reciprocal. But even if it isn't and it turns out that the other person is attached, a good flirt will still leave them feeling complimented rather than offended.

Flirting doesn't involve 'dumbing down' either. Quite the contrary. Flirting involves skill: the ability to articulate feelings, the intuition to pick up on what makes people tick, the courage to delve below the usual superficial level of conversation, and a great deal of judgement to know when it's appropriate to tease, when to back off, when to plant your foot on the accelerator and just go for it. The cleverer the person, the better flirt they make. So if you think it's beneath your dignity or intelligence, think again. It takes more than a pair of batting eyelashes or smarmy compliments to qualify for the Flirt of the Year award.

FLIRTING? OR JUST BEING FRIENDLY?

The question that I'm most often asked is: 'How do I know if someone's flirting with me?' Unfortunately, it isn't that easy to work out if they are flirting or just being incredibly friendly, especially if it's a stranger. Some people flirt so often, they do it in their sleep. They don't care if it's a man, woman, dog, cat or insect: if it's got a pulse, they'll flirt with it. So, if someone like this aims some hair-flicking your way, it's probably not a good idea to spend too much time tossing up whether to have the fish or the chicken at the wedding reception. It could mean absolutely nothing.

For someone else, who might be quite shy, simply standing still and talking to you is their equivalent of flirting outrageously. So there's that problem: are they always like this or is this just for me? When you've got that sorted out, another question immediately pops up: what sort of flirting is it? What's their intention? Is it a bit of harmless hair-flicking, designed to give both of you an ego boost and a giggle? Are they thinking a your-place-or-mine scenario, or maybe a clasp-hands-and-run-towards-the-sunset situation? Is it any wonder a lot of us think 'Oh, I give up' at this point and head straight for the bar? (This will confuse the issue even further. You think your judgement's bad now, wait until you've had a couple.)

Unfortunately, it's impossible for me to give you a foolproof guide that will always turn up the correct result on whether someone's flirting with you or not. People are far too individual for that. But I can give you some pretty good tips, which should point you in the right direction. These work hand in hand with the five sure signs of interest (see pages 44–6).

TIP 1:

FORGET ABOUT WHAT THEY'RE SAYING – FOCUS ENTIRELY ON THEIR BODY LANGUAGE

If possible, let them rattle on while you have a good look at what's going on. Are they waving their hands a lot, fidgeting with their clothes, gazing over your shoulder? All these things signify something, but not necessarily what you think (more on that later).

TIP 2:

CHECK YOUR OWN BODY LANGUAGE

Are you giving off the right signals to the person you're interested in? Are you facing them, with your body squared towards them? Are you sending the right eye contact signals? Standing close? Leaning forward with your upper body? Remember the Seven Deadly Body Language Sins on pages 20–5 and make sure you're not guilty of any of them.

TIP 3: LOOK AT THE OTHER PERSON'S BODY LANGUAGE
AND APPLY THE RULE OF FOUR

To be pretty certain someone fancies you, they must show a minimum of four positive body language signals (directed at you rather than the gorgeous blonde/hunk standing beside or behind you).

TIP 4: DELIBERATELY CHANGE YOUR POSITION TO SEE
IF THEY FOLLOW YOU

This is called mirroring (see page 45): if we're keen on someone, we try to stay on the same level as them. So if you change your position, they should follow by imitating whatever new posture you've adopted. A word of warning here: make sure you don't do this too abruptly or shift into negative body language or they'll think you're suddenly not interested. People mirror bad body language as well as good, so if you suddenly sit back, cross your arms and look down your nose, chances are they'll think the game is over and do the same. Instead, try something like leaning over and swirling a straw in your drink/placing a hand, palm down, on top of the table closer to their side than yours. These are things they could easily mirror if they wanted to, without looking silly.

TIP 5: FLIRT MORE INTENSELY

The best way to find out if they're flirting with you is to flirt back. At this point, forget being subtle; intensify all your body language signals. Try leaning in really, really close and see if they lean in to join you. Touch them on their upper arm and leave your fingers there for a minute or so. Do they pull away or seem comfortable with your touch? Wait for a pause in the conversation, then hold their eye contact for four seconds, looking sexily at them, without saying a word. Then let a slow smile spread across your face. This very obviously says 'I think we're flirting' without you having to say it out loud. If they smile back and continue doing all they have been, you're on the home run. If, however, they make an excuse and leave at this point, they were flirting for fun, not end result, and you just upped the odds to over-serious stakes. (Never mind, better to find out early than late.) If all else fails and they still don't ask for your phone number when you're about to part, ask for theirs. Their reticence could simply be a case of shyness or thinking you're way out of their league.

FLIRTING FOR BOYS

Answers to your most commonly asked questions (well, the ones I can print anyway).

I'M IN A BUSY BAR WHERE THERE ARE PLENTY OF SINGLE WOMEN. HOW DO I KNOW WHICH ONES I STAND A CHANCE WITH?

Sit somewhere that you can discreetly check out the talent and watch what the different groups of girls are doing. Are they perched on stools, anxiously scanning the crowd, not chatting terribly much and looking hopefully into the faces of any passing guy? These girls are more than a safe bet – they're desperate. Quasimodo could ask them to dance and they'd accept. The cute little foursome who are talking animatedly together but still glance up if a nice-looking guy walks past? They're interested and probably interesting as well: although they're probably out to meet someone, it's not the entire evening's entertainment. As a basic rule, the more interest she's paying to her surroundings rather than her friend, the more open she is to being approached. Well, sort of. Women have this in-built polite gene which makes them continue to listen and nod and smile at their friend's he-said-then-I-said stories when really they're dying to glance over at the cute guy near the bar. So don't discount them: just be aware you need some sort of distraction ploy for the friend.

I'VE SPOTTED A LIKELY CONTENDER. NOW WHAT?

Try making eye contact from a distance and see if she smiles or looks back. It's still the best indicator of all that she's interested. Make eye contact while smiling at her and hold for a count of one, two, three, four, then drop your eyes and smile to yourself, then look up again two seconds later. If she's still looking at you or looks back within a few seconds, she's interested. Either that or her longed-for ex-boyfriend is standing behind you. Not sure you're ready to risk being so upfront by walking straight to her side? If she's not giving you much feedback, and you're not sure if she's playing cool and mysterious or just not interested, find some excuse to walk past, very gently brush her arm or somehow touch her and see what happens then. Invariably, she'll meet your eyes and have one of two reactions: amusement (I know that was just an excuse to touch me and get my attention) or disdain (ditto but basically clear off). Take your cue from there.

IT'S ALL GOING WONDERFULLY WELL BUT SHE'S ABOUT TO TAKE HER JACKET OFF AND – OH MY GOD! – WHERE DO I LOOK IF HER BREASTS ARE...WELL, RATHER IMPRESSIVE?

Don't panic for a start. Believe me, if they're that impressive, she's expecting some sort of reaction when she takes her jacket off. Which is where Andy went wrong. Andy, from Leeds, was on his dummy date when his date peeled off an outer layer of clothes to reveal an enviable cleavage. Terrified he'd be branded sleazy if he so much as registered the fact, Andy kept his eyes firmly trained on her face and refused to look below that level for the rest of the date. Admirable, but he missed a brilliant opportunity to relate to her as a date rather than as a friend – which was the problem. Now, while Andy obviously scored big brownie points by not spending the evening with eyes on stalks, gazing down her cleavage (as you will too), it's also not a terribly good idea to completely ignore it. The correct breast protocol (I can't believe I'm writing this) is to acknowledge them, compliment, then move on. The equivalent of the polite meet-greet-quick-shake-of-hands thing. Imagine the girl attached to the breasts is saying something like this: 'John, I don't think you've met Mary and Jane before, have you? Well, Mary, Jane, this is John. What's that? They're good-looking girls? Yes, they are pretty aren't they? Anyway, as I was saying...'

Get the idea? Right, here's how. When she takes her top off, it's quite normal to let your eyes run over those curves and say something like 'Wow! You've got a great figure. I'm sorry, I know you must hear that all the time but you're in great shape. That outfit looks fantastic on you – but then again, anything would look fantastic on you.' Note emphasis on 'great figure' (as opposed to 'great breasts'), and 'great shape' (as opposed to 'great chest') and the comment at the end about the whole outfit looking great (as opposed to just the part stretched across the good bits). It's the perfect balance of a.) you've got great knockers, b.) but I bet you're sick of men telling you that and staring at them so c.) let's move on because it's not just your breasts I find interesting but all of you. Then – and this bit's crucial if you're to carry this off – you really must move on. Don't stare. Keep the conversation going. Don't try to sneak peeks when she's not looking.

IS IT A GOOD IDEA TO TOUCH HER TO SHOW I'M INTERESTED? OR SHOULD I WAIT FOR HER TO TOUCH ME FIRST?

As a general rule, the first person to touch sends the first 'I'm keen on you' signal. Most women know this and don't want to appear pushy or 'easy', so they'll often put their hands or arms or legs deliberately near yours so that it's easy for you to touch them. Alternatively, they'll put them somewhere that you'll accidentally touch them. So if she's got her hands seemingly in the way or quite close, especially if they're on the table and sort of over your side, she's keen.

When you first touch depends on the situation. Maybe if you end up going on somewhere else and you're walking along, you might touch her to grab her attention and point something out; or you might take her hand before crossing a busy street (and don't let go). It's a great idea to find some sort of excuse to touch her because, as I'm terribly fond of saying, even one brief touch can have a dramatic effect on the way we feel about someone. I was out boy-shopping in Wales recently, where we were filming *WLTM* at a rugby club (I know, getting paid to flirt with gorgeous men is such hard work…). Anyway, the fact is that the entire team were so gob-smackingly gorgeous, it was difficult to know who to focus our attention on. Then this guy came up, introduced himself, looked me straight in the eye and simultaneously put his hand in the small of my back to move me closer so he could hear my name properly. One single touch and I instantly decided he was the one I wanted to get to know better.

OK, WE'VE NOW BEEN ON SEVERAL DATES. WHAT KIND OF SIGNALS DOES SHE GIVE IF SHE'S READY TO (AHEM) MOVE THINGS FURTHER?

By 'further' I assume you mean sexually? The answer to that is easy: wait until you're both well aware of what having sex will mean to you both. If you're a nice guy (and of course you are), but one night of frenzied sheet-shredding is all you're after, let her know. Even if you have to lie. Say something like, 'Look, I think you should know that I've just come out of a long-term relationship/I'm really busy at work right now/I'm about to trek across Nepal and I'm not interested in a serious, committed relationship. I think you're gorgeous and I'd love to have fun with you but if you're looking for more, I'm the wrong person.' Sure, some women will instantly exit stage left. But there are plenty of women who are also interested in nothing more than no-strings sex, so it's not a given that she'll knock you back. At least this way she knows the score and you're not subjected to her sending boiled bunny rabbits *Fatal Attraction*-style, through the post.

If you think she might be 'The One' (or at least a potential candidate) and you're open to seeing where it leads you both, I'd give it about four dates. Then, during an appropriately hot, teenage-style petting session, say something like, 'I'm desperate to make love to you. I don't mean do the full bit but I'd certainly like to take it further. Is it too soon for you?' Leave it more than four dates to make some sort of move and she'll start thinking you're more George Michael than George Clooney. Or she'll embark on the Cabbage Diet because she thinks she's too fat and you don't fancy her. (And believe me, you do not want her on the Cabbage Diet.) By asking if it's too soon for her, she's also got the message you're not just out for 'one thing', and when you do make love, it probably means the start of something rather than the finish. She's special enough for you to wait.

CAN'T FIGURE WOMEN OUT?

Here are three quick and sneaky ways to get the inside story on what makes women tick. (We're not that difficult, honest.) **Flick through a glossy**. Choose a magazine that seems to aim at the type of women you find attractive, pretend you're buying it for your sister/girlfriend, then settle in for a good read. Women's mags are packed with loads of secret stuff women tell each other but not men.

Spend the day watching telly. Girlie telly. It's another great way to get insights into what makes women tick. Some good video choices are *Sex and the City*, *Friends*, *Ally McBeal* or *Linda Green*.

Hang out with women as much as possible. Do this preferably in non-dating, non-threatening environments (the supermarket, the gym, your sister's birthday party). The more you hang around women, the more you will see that we're just like you, with a few different bits. Yes, there are a lot of surface differences between the sexes, but dig deep enough and you'll hit middle ground. Underneath it all we've got the same dreams, needs, desires, fears and anxieties as you have. The quicker you realize this, the less scary women will seem and the more naturally you will behave around them (always a good thing). The more you surround yourself with women, the quicker you'll come to this conclusion.

HOMEWORK:

STEP OUT OF YOUR COMFORT ZONE

The idea behind this exercise is to get you used to chatting comfortably with strange women (as in women you don't know, rather than women who are plain odd). On *WLTM* I sent George off to deliver a 'You've got a great smile' compliment to two girls in a pub in the city. Much as he claimed to be 'a typical Greek guy' with 'the gift of the gab', approaching a stranger in a bar and saying anything (let alone giving a compliment) was nail-bitingly stressful for him. The thing is, though, once he'd done it (albeit circling a few times, clutching our drinks, before he moved in for the kill), the fear evaporated and afterwards it was easy for him to talk to strangers. Another infamous *WLTM* contributor was Jon – a 41-year-old former journalist from Plymouth who was incredibly articulate and intelligent. Jon had no problems pitching ideas in a business sense but quaked in his leather trousers when forced to chat up a woman. Getting up the courage to approach girls in a bar and deliver a compliment – just as George and Jon did on *WLTM* – can feel like the most difficult thing in the world, but they both did it and felt great afterwards. So how about giving it a try yourself? Yes, you will feel like a twit to begin with, but when you've done it once, there'll be no stopping you.

It's about mega-quick chats rather than long, intense conversations that involve you swapping phone numbers. So don't be too fussy about who you target, OK? You're giving them a compliment, not asking if they'll have your babies. This exercise works best if you're out with a friend or group of friends because it relies on moving purposefully back to where you came from. This is a bit hard to do if all you were doing was leaning up against a wall on your own. Here's how it works:

- Go to the bar, get a drink and have a look around to spot any female you're interested in. Smile and catch her eye (note 'her' not 'their': you're only allowed one at a time), then look away. Buy at least two drinks: one for you, one for your friend(s). You're not going to look like a come-on if it's obvious you have to deliver drinks back to the table.
- Go in her direction on the way back to your table. Smile and catch her eye again as you approach.
- Just before you reach her, pause for one second when you're close enough to eavesdrop (pretend something or someone has distracted you for an instant). What you're now doing is getting a 'mood sound bite' (i.e. checking she's not talking about her ex just dumping her or about having to put her dog down).

- If it feels safe to proceed, walk up to her and say, 'Excuse me, but I couldn't help coming over to you to tell you…' (Pay her a compliment you feel comfortable giving and that's suitable for the circumstances. 'You've got such a great smile' is appropriate. 'If ever you want to put your shoes under my bed, you'd be welcome' isn't.)
- As you're delivering the compliment, pretend she's an old friend you haven't seen for years and that you're genuinely chuffed to have run into her. (Decide on who you'll pretend this is before you make the walk over. This way your face will soften and you'll come across as more interested and friendly than slimy or sleazy.)
- Once you've delivered your line say, 'Well, nice talking to you. I'd better deliver these.' Gesture to the drinks, then walk back to your friend(s).

There! Now how easy was that?

FLIRTING FOR GIRLS

Where to meet men, what to do when you find them and where to meet more if you're not happy with the first lot.

I NEVER SEEM TO MEET ELIGIBLE, AVAILABLE MEN. WHERE ARE THEY ALL?

Please don't tell me you do that classic sad, single girl thing of spending most Friday and Saturday nights having dinner with your couple friends? You do? Oh, puhleeze! Now tell me: do they invite single Brad Pitt lookalikes along for you? Are they in the habit of hiding single men in the kitchen cupboard, under the fridge and in the bathroom? No such luck? Then why are you surprised you're not meeting any men? Where do you think you're going to meet the man of your dreams if you don't go anywhere to meet new people? Is he going to suddenly appear from under the sofa while you're watching telly? Unless you get lucky with the pizza delivery boy, it ain't going to happen. You've got to get out there, girl. (Jeremy has lots of ideas about suitable places, see page 113.)

From now on, you're banned from going to friends' houses for dinner on Friday and Saturday nights. You can go during the week but not at weekends. Weekends are boy-shopping nights. (I'll make an exception if they've invited someone dishy and single along.) And another thing: boy-shopping doesn't just happen on weekend nights. Yes, I did just say Friday and Saturday nights are boy-shopping nights, but so are Monday, Tuesday, Wednesday and Thursday – day and nights by the way. And let's not forget Sunday. (No rest for the wicked.)

What I want you to realize is this: you don't just meet potential dates in a bar. In fact, that's often the last place you meet them. So stop thinking you need to be in a bar or club and three sheets to the wind to meet someone. You've got the potential to meet a guy in the ordinary places you go to all the time, such as the supermarket. And you're not exactly going to be hovering around the household cleaners aisle in your little black dress after three gin and tonics, are you? That's my point. You don't need be 'done up' and looking your best to meet someone, and you don't have to be drunk to approach a guy either. All you need is attitude, confidence and courage – the three qualities this book (and the TV programme) is all about. I want you to get into the habit of approaching guys at every opportunity. In the sandwich place at lunchtime. On the train platform. In the chemist. At the newsagent's. Walking in the park. Nowhere is sacred. The entire world has just become your dating ground. (Lucky you!)

AM I BETTER OFF HANGING OUT FOR MR RIGHT
OR SHOULD I DATE WHOEVER ASKS ME OUT AS PRACTISE?

Dating is like everything else in life: the more practise you have, the better you are at it. Which is exactly what I told Kelly, a *WLTM* contributor with a body honed to perfection from a lifetime of sport – and a distinctly hostile attitude to any guy who dared to look at it. Kelly would happily push a sleeve up to arm-wrestle any guy in the pub but she refused to date a man unless he was her idea of Mr Perfect. Boy-shopping with Kelly was extraordinary – men were dismissed for all sorts of defects such as the wrong ears, the way he lifted his beer glass or the way he raised his eyebrows. Yes, we did laugh an awful lot on the night because her perception of people was very funny, but the end result was that Kelly felt pretty terrible at the end of it, because she hadn't found a final date. There's another good reason to flirt with/date a million Mr Wrongs before settling on just one: pheromones – those subtle chemicals we secrete to attract each other. Ever noticed how much sexier you feel when you've been out and been chatted up a lot? It's not just your confidence that's been boosted, it's your pheromone level. Even better if you've had a snog (or more) because then not only do your pheromone levels get nicely stimulated, you absorb some of the guy's through your skin, which tops you up even more.

If you're having regular sex, you're sexier. It's a fact. The more sex you have, the more sex you want. The more you feel like sex, the sexier you are because you're exuding pheromones, which people are subconsciously attracted to. That's why one wicked weekend away can make all the difference. Now I'm not condoning casual sex or suggesting you drag the milkman in by the scruff of his neck the next time he innocently pops a pint on your front doorstep, but I am suggesting you do the next best thing, which is to flirt like there's no tomorrow. And if you happen to have a snog with someone while you're at it, well, that would be quite a good idea.

WHAT ARE SOME OBVIOUS SEXY SIGNALS I CAN SEND TO SHOW
I'M INTERESTED WITHOUT, WELL, SEEMING TOO OBVIOUS?

Wear high heels: Women worry about the size of their bums, but bums that stick out are consistently judged as sexier than little bums that don't. High heels, on average, make your bottom protrude by 25 per cent more. Emphasis on the word 'protrude' as opposed to 'make bum look bigger'. (If you really want to make him sit up and pay attention, team the heels with a pair of tightish jeans and put your hand in the back pocket.)

Give shoe signals: Shoes say a lot about our sexual mood. Sometimes we'll slip our foot in and out of a shoe (no prizes for guessing what you're secretly thinking when you're doing that one), or we'll dangle it on the tip of our toes (keeping him dangling at the same time).

Cross your legs: When you cross and uncross your legs in front of a guy, you are interested in him. (I believe they teach this to men in infant school.)

Combine all the above: Want to see him really sweat? One of the strongest, most deliberate and most obvious sexual messages a woman can give a man is as follows. Cross your legs while holding eye contact and turned toward him. Next, let your high heel shoe drop until it's dangling from your toe. Then begin to slowly and seductively kick your foot up and down in a thrusting (get the picture?) motion. Note, this only works with sexy high heels. The effect is dampened somewhat if you attempt it with trainers or sensible flatties. (Sorry, but I didn't promise comfort along with flirtability.)

WHAT IF I'M IN A CROWDED BAR, CAN'T SIT DOWN OR HE CAN SEE ONLY THE TOP HALF OF ME?

If that's the case, it's time for some touch-and-tease techniques. Flirting ploys like these have been around for ever (think Marilyn), but whoever said you can have too much of a good thing was wrong in this instance. The following are variations of techniques suggested by Barbara Keesling (author of *The Good Girl's Guide to Bad Girl Sex*). Sue, a gorgeous blonde widow who appeared on *WLTM*, scoffed and wouldn't take me seriously when I first tried to teach her these techniques – they were 'too contrived', felt 'unnatural' and were way over-the-top. But the whole idea of all the flirting techniques I talk about in this book and on the programme, is that you take the principle behind them and experiment with what works for you. Tone them down if it all feels too much – turn them up if you feel it's not enough. Interestingly, in Sue's case, the 'too girly' criticism disappeared out of the window (almost as fast as Jay's makeover transformed her from Ms Dungaree to Madonna) when faced with a guy she fancied the pants off on her final date. Anyway, these techniques are yours to try out and play with to see what suits you:

Touch-and-tease ploy 1: While he's talking, stroke your left collar-bone three times with the ring finger of your right hand. Maintain eye contact with him as you're doing it and let your hand rest there when you've finished.

Touch-and-tease ploy 2: Throw your head back slightly (it'll look more natural if you wait until the next time you laugh) and move your hand to the base of your throat. Now slowly, ever so slowly, let your fingers slide down your throat towards your breasts. Stop just where your cleavage starts and let your fingers rest there. Keep them there as long as he talks, but when you talk, remove your hand. Can you think of a better incentive for him to keep talking to you?

Touch-and-tease ploy 3: Now I want you to visualize what it would be like to kiss this guy. While you're conjuring up a scenario in your head, look at him and slowly stroke your bottom lip with your index finger. If you can carry it off, lower your head slightly as you're looking at him. What does this do? It makes him wonder what on earth is going through your head because it's quite obviously something naughty but he doesn't know you well enough to ask outright. To really seal the deal, say something like, 'Sorry, what were you saying? I got a bit lost there.' This is particularly effective if he was saying something he considered you'd be mega-interested in (like the fact that he owns a private jet). By the way, it's crucial with this one that you maintain eye contact or it sends the opposite signal – that you drifted off because you were bored.

Does this all sound a bit contrived and girly for you? As I told the reluctant Sue, I deliberately overplay and exaggerate all the body language gestures and ploys so that it's blatantly clear what I'm getting at. The idea is for you to play around with them, see what feels comfortable and what doesn't, and adapt them to suit. If you'd prefer to skip straight to the simplified, less vampy versions, give these a go.

Cheat's version of touch-and-tease ploy 1: Instead of stroking your collar-bone, simply hold your hand there. Splay your fingers and lift your hand so just the tips of your fingers touch.

Cheat's version of touch-and-tease ploy 2: Instead of sliding your fingers down your throat toward your cleavage, stroke the hollow of your throat instead.

Cheat's version of touch-and-tease ploy 3: Can't bring yourself to stroke your bottom lip? Look at the guy's mouth instead while he's talking.

ANY OTHER GREAT IDEAS FOR WHERE TO GO TO MEET MEN AND PRACTISE ALL THIS STUFF?

The following pick-up pointers are tried and tested. Lots of them worked on the show, so I can't see any reason why they won't work for you.

- If you want to meet men en masse, get yourself along to a car show. Drape yourself across the bonnet of a sports car (under the guise of peering through the windscreen) and he'll stop admiring the sleek curves of the car and start admiring yours. It's easy to start up a conversation. Say, 'She's beautiful, isn't she?' (referring to the car) and with a bit of luck he'll come back with, 'And so are you.' (Yes, it's cheesy, but it still gives the old ego a ridiculous boost if delivered from the right pair of lips.) Of course, if you really want male attention guaranteed permanently, buy yourself a sports car.

- Forget chatrooms (you can't see what he looks like). The best way to cyberdate is to get yourself down to an Internet café. Slide into the computer next to the cutest guy in the place and check him out surreptitiously by sneaking a peek at what he's writing or reading on the screen. You can tell a lot about someone by the sites they visit while surfing the Net – better still if he's e-mailing a friend. How to get his attention? Play dumb. You've never surfed the Net before ('I know, hard to believe but true,' delivered with a slightly embarrassed grimace). A really good flirt will deliberately give herself away within five minutes (I never said you had to play dumb for ever) by catching on just a little too fast. At this point, you come clean by confessing, 'OK, I might have done it, well, thousands of times. But how else was I supposed to get your attention?' Say it with a cheeky yes-we-both-know-you-would-have-noticed-me-anyway look, and you're hardly wearing your heart on your sleeve, are you?

- Borrow a friend's dog (choose exceptionally cute or exceptionally ugly because either attracts attention) and take it with you to an outdoor café or bar, to the shops or to the park. (It worked a treat for Andy on *WLTM*, so there's no reason why it won't work for you too.) A pet gives him a great excuse to talk to you – and it weeds out the nice guys from the not-so-nice. A million surveys have shown that animal lovers are kinder, gentler and far more loyal than those who aren't interested in our four-legged friends. If he can resist giving the pooch a pat, chances are he's not worth picking up.

- Kid yourself into taking a risk. Pretend you've just bought a one-way ticket to the other side of the world. You've got nothing to lose if you're not going to be around, and you'll be far more likely to be pro-active.

- Turn grocery shopping into a datefest. Single guys have to eat (they don't all exist on McDonalds – although the frozen food aisle is probably a better bet than the fresh fruit and vegetable section). If you choose your time and place carefully, there are more dates to be had at the supermarket than the local bar.

THANKS BUT NO THANKS

LETTING YOUR BODY SAY 'I'M NOT INTERESTED' WITHOUT APPEARING RUDE

Constantly getting chatted up by guys you don't fancy to the point where you miss out on those you do? Here's how to make sure you don't spend the entire

HOMEWORK:

FIND YOUR FLIRTING STYLE

Try out the 'touch and tease' exercises in front of the mirror, until you hit on a version which looks best for you. The next step is to practise it in real life. Target a (very lucky) stranger the next time you're out, and try delivering a very tame version. Turn the volume up with other guys as the night goes on, depending on how confident you feel – and how much you fancy the guy on the receiving end!

Are you too picky? Do a reality check. Pinpoint three friends you consider to be on the same level of attractiveness as you. How many dates do you go on, compared to them? Do you consider yourself fussier than they are? If they've been on six dates in the period of time it takes for you to agree to have a coffee with someone, you're being too picky. At the same time think about your attached friends who seem blissfully happy. Are their partners textbook perfect: good-looking, rich and all-round perfect? Didn't think so. Do you really care whether the guy who made your friend Anna happy isn't perhaps who you'd initially have matched her up with? Moral of the story: it's not about the exterior package, it's the person inside that counts.

evening making polite chit-chat without turning into Ms Bitch. It's all a matter of positioning your body the right way.

Use a block. Shut out the person by putting some sort of physical object between you and them. On a bus, you might lift the newspaper after someone makes meaningful eye contact, or raise the menu in a restaurant. Assuming you don't then play a game of peekaboo and keep lowering the block to stare at him, he'll get the hint. If you're standing up or don't have something to use as a barrier, use your body instead. Simply turn away from him. Even if you angle your body slightly away, it's an unwelcoming gesture.

Use a barrier. This is less obvious than blocking, so if your polite gene is in overdrive, this is the technique for you. Barriers are more 'I'm not entirely convinced you're interesting but you could convince me if you tried hard' than 'Forget it'. But they still send a mild chill through the air rather than a gushy, warm, welcoming vibe. The most obvious barrier is crossing your arms. If you're mildly uninterested, keep them quite loosely crossed with your fingers splayed and on show. If you're really not interested, fold them tightly and clench your fists or hold on to your arms above the elbows in a tight clasp. (By the way, be careful that all this arm-crossing and clenching doesn't produce a rather spectacular cleavage, or it'll have the opposite effect to the one you want.)

Avoid eye contact. If a guy does manage to catch your eye, keep it to one or two seconds. If you must, acknowledge you've noticed him looking at you by giving a quick polite nod. Don't let your eyes drop below eye level, and whatever you do, don't look at his mouth or body.

Don't smile. Even a tight, closed-mouth smile will be interpreted as encouragement to come and talk to you. Having said that, if you feel obliged to return a smile, this is the sort you should reciprocate with.

FIVE SURE SIGNS THEY (OR YOU) ARE INTERESTED

OK, now we're really getting down to the nitty-gritty – the five fundamentals of flirting. While flirting gestures and body language can differ between the sexes, most of them aren't gender specific. This means you're both dead keen if you do any of the following.

SURE SIGN 1: EYE CONTACT IS DIRECT, DELIBERATE AND LINGERING

Most human beings scan each other's faces for three seconds at a time. Natural curiosity makes us connect and glance at each other's features. If we pause for more than three seconds, it usually means we're interested.

Someone's keen if: You/they look for four and a half seconds or more. It doesn't sound that much longer but it feels like it when that gaze is directed at you.

Someone's really keen if: The crucial four-and-a-half-second look is repeated twice in quick succession. It happens once, the eyes look away, but return to the person's face almost immediately to repeat the experience. Once says 'I've noticed you'. Several times means 'I'm interested – are you?'

SURE SIGN 2: THE EYES FOLLOW A TRIANGULAR PATH

This is called the flirting triangle. In a business situation, our eyes make a zigzag motion across someone's face: we look from eye to eye and across the bridge of the nose. With friends, the look drops below eye level: we still look from eye to eye but also include the nose and mouth to make a triangle shape.

Someone's keen if: The triangle expands. The more we fancy someone, the bigger the triangle gets, but this time it widens at the bottom to include their good bits (i.e. most interesting boy and girl body parts).

Someone's really keen if: The eye contact is intense and goes from eye to eye, and more time is spent looking at the mouth. If someone is watching your mouth while you're talking to them, it's very, very sexy because you can't help but think 'I wonder if they're imagining what it would be like to kiss me'. In fact, this is usually exactly what they're thinking if their gaze lingers on your mouth.

SURE
SIGN 3:   YOU MIRROR EACH OTHER

They do whatever you seem to or vice versa. It's called mirroring and is what separates a good flirt from a great flirt. Nothing will bond you more instantly or effectively than imitating someone's behaviour.

Someone's keen if: They lean forward to tell you something intimate and you lean in to meet them. If they sit back to take a sip of their drink and look you in the eye, you take a sip of your drink and do the same. They sit with their chin cupped in their hands, so do you. The theory behind mirroring is that we like people who are like us. If someone is doing what we're doing, we feel they're on the same level as us and in the same mood as we are.

Someone's really keen if: You deliberately change your posture/stance or whatever you're doing and the person you're with 'mirrors' you within a minute or so. They're very keen to 'stay with you' in all senses.

SURE
SIGN 4:   YOU'RE RAISING EYEBROWS

When we first see someone we're attracted to, our eyebrows rise and fall. If they fancy us back, they raise their eyebrows in return. Never noticed? It's not surprising since the whole thing lasts about a fifth of a second. We're not consciously aware of doing it, but it's a gesture that is duplicated by every culture on earth. In fact, some experts claim it's the most instantly recognized non-verbal sign of friendly greeting in the world.

Someone's keen if: They raise their eyebrows on first meeting you, so watch for it when you meet someone you fancy.

Someone's really keen if: The eyebrow lift is extended for up to one second. For maximum impact, do this while making full eye contact.

YOU'RE PLAYING FOOTSY

Yes, I admit it, on the show I come across as a woman obsessed with feet. Nothing gets me more excited than seeing two pairs of 'final date' feet snuggling and pointing very obviously in each other's direction. (Second biggest excitement: if they share dessert as well.) Well, there's a reason for my foot fetish: most of the action really does happen under the table. Our feet and hands point towards the person we're interested in – it's that simple. In the *WLTM* van, one camera is nearly always trained purely on the dummy/final date feet formation. Why? Nothing else gives a quicker, more effective mood reading of what's happening on the date than how the feet are placed. Is one of them wishing like mad they could run away? Check out the feet and they're already pointing to the nearest exit. Do they seem to have forgotten the cameras (and us hidden 'experts') and look settled in for the evening? Both sets of tootsies are facing each other, inching closer as we watch.

Someone's keen if: Their feet are pointing at you. This is particularly clear in a group situation, where the feet unconsciously indicate who fancies whom. The signal is often picked up by the person it's directed at without them really knowing why. So if you're got your eye on the hunk/hunkette in the corner, point your feet in their direction. Even if you don't make eye contact, they'll subliminally get the hint that you're interested.

Someone's really keen if: It's not just the feet pointing towards the person. If we're really keen, we'll 'point' subconsciously with hands, arms, eyes, legs, feet and toes. Other male body parts may also be involved…

SLOW TO GET THE MESSAGE?

Try dropping these hints that you'd like to do more than share a cab home…

- Lots of people kiss on the cheek to say goodbye to someone they've just met and got on well with. Most people air kiss, but some do kiss the cheek and it lasts about three-quarters of a second. If you extend this by just half a second, so it's one and a quarter seconds long, the non-verbal message is clear. It's, 'I fancy you and I want to kiss you more.'
- Back up your parting compliment/invitation for coffee with the lethal threesome. Say your piece while 1.) leaning in close, 2.) smiling and 3.) holding eye contact. Do all three simultaneously and you'll intensify the whole thing by 300 per cent.

THE 10 GOLDEN RULES OF BOY- AND GIRL- SHOPPING

If you haven't seen the television programme, you're probably wondering what on earth I'm on about with this 'boy/girl-shopping' bit. The truth is, the term was invented during the making of the pilot show. I was just about to take our very first *WLTM* star out on the town to find her a man, and frantically compiling a list of all Mr Ideal's must-haves in my head because I so wanted to find him for her. Suddenly I thought, 'Blimey! If I'm feeling under pressure, she must be terrified. I bet she wishes we were going shopping instead.' And then I thought, 'But we are going shopping. I've got the shopping list after all.' So instead of saying, 'Come on! Let's go out on the pull' when the cameras starting rolling, I blurted out, 'Let's go boy-shopping!' Everyone (including me) looked a bit startled, then we all laughed and the term just stuck. If you think it's politically incorrect or disrespectful, I'm sorry, but it's just meant to be funny and make the business of meeting someone seem less intimidating too.

Right, now back to the fun part. Boy/girl-shopping can be done anywhere, anytime, solo or with a friend. It's the chance to put all the techniques you've learnt about into practise, and if you stick to the following rules, you never know what bargains you'll find.

RULE 1:   BE FLEXIBLE

We've all got a 'type' but it's a bit drastic restricting yourself to blondes with long legs and perfect teeth or tanned men with hair-free chests, elegant hands and a left eyebrow slightly higher than the right. (Don't laugh – you should hear some people's wishlists.) In most cases, the person we end up blissfully happy with doesn't come packaged quite the way we thought. The more you force yourself to chat to people who don't automatically fit your 'perfection profile', the more chance you have of finding a good match (there's strength in numbers, if nothing else).

Ideally, your shopping list won't have any physical must-haves on it at all (emphasis on word 'ideally'). At least try to base it mainly on qualities that really do matter (trust, loyalty, intelligence, sense of humour). I'm not suggesting for a moment that you compromise on personality or morality issues, but I am suggesting that looks, money and/or possessions aren't the great indicators of future happiness and compatibility you might think they are. So take a second look, be open to seeing past the exterior packaging and you might surprise yourself. On the other hand, if you meet someone who soooooooo does it for you that you don't care if they're rich/poor/earthling or alien, don't discount them either. I'm the first to admit the truth of the next rule.

RULE 2: CHEMISTRY COUNTS

When we first meet someone, we have an instant reaction to whether we fancy them or not. It's called chemistry. This can take a while to develop, so it's worth hanging around, just for a short time, to see if it happens with someone new. On the other hand, if it feels like someone's just thumped you in the middle of your chest and all the clichés like 'weak at the knees' suddenly make sense, you've hit the jackpot. Chemistry like this is rare and extremely powerful. Usually it's based on physical attraction, so it tends to disappear once you both emerge from the bedroom (even if it is 10 years later). Sometimes, though, it's backed up by other, more enduring attributes, such as getting on outside the bedroom as well as in it. In that case, hang on tight. Chemistry is what keeps couples going through the really rough times: it's stronger than superglue and 300 billion times more binding than a marriage certificate.

RULE 3: GO SHOPPING IN PLACES YOU LIKE

It seems logical to me but you're not really going to be looking, sounding or acting your best if you're somewhere you'd really rather not be. If you think singles bars are horrible, desperate places, you're not that big on drinking or dancing, and hate chatting up strangers, what are you doing there? What do you have in common with the other people who've chosen to come to that venue? Not all are fellow sufferers also thinking, 'Please, God, let me find someone tonight so I never have to come here again.' Think outside the box for boy/girl-shopping. Don't think 'Where can I go to meet a date?' Think 'What would I like to learn about and explore in my life?' This has instant advantages: you're more comfortable and relaxed in an environment you belong in, which makes you more approachable, and your prime purpose isn't just to meet someone, which rather effectively removes that air of desperation (about as attractive as BO).

RULE 4: SORT OUT YOUR FRIENDS

If you've got the choice between going out on your own or taking your best friend along, you'd have to be daft to opt for going it alone. But trying to pull when that friend's glaring at potentials like a slightly rabid Rottweiler is a bit like trying to run a marathon with weights strapped to your ankles. If your friend's a tad over-protective, pull them aside and have a little chat. Make an agreement: if one of you starts talking to someone you like, the other nips off to the loo or to get a drink. This gives you a five-minute window to say to someone, 'Look, I'm here with my best friend/girlfriend and don't want to desert her/him, so if

I seem like I'm not interested in talking to just you alone, that's why. I'm just trying to make them feel included as well.' If you're really keen add, 'Please don't rush off without giving me a way to contact you because that would be tragic. I can't wait to have you all to myself.' (The only thing more off-putting than an over-protective friend is a pack of them. Even if the natives aren't drunk and seem friendly, it's daunting enough making a possible fool of yourself chatting up one person. Only a superhero would attempt it with five other pairs of eyes looking on. Hunt in packs and you'll invariably all end up empty-handed.)

RULE 5: DON'T CLOSE YOURSELF OFF

Got the venue, friends and attitude right, but still aren't having any luck attracting attention? Check that your body language is giving off the right signals. Mentally distance yourself a few feet away and consider yourself from the standpoint of a potential date. If your spine is stiff and rigid, your arms are folded across your chest and you're leaning back on the bar looking bored, you could be saying 'This place is more fun than *Sex and the City*' but the message is still going to be 'I'm not enjoying myself'. Another way to ensure that no one comes near you is to cover your tummy with your arms, coat, menu, magazine or pillow. The rest of the room really isn't noticing you're having a fat day, but people are subconsciously responding to the barrier you're putting between you and them.

RULE 6: ADJUST YOUR VOLUME CONTROL

Most of us have multiple personalities. At any given moment there are several people in there, all jostling for attention. What to do on a night off? The shy shoe-shuffler side of us wants to flake out in front of a video. The attention-seeking party-goer says, 'Oh, don't be such a wimp! Let's head for a bar.' The sensible /intellectual person inside us tut-tuts and says, 'You know what you should do: stay at work and clear the backlog.' In normal, stress-free situations we let a little of each person shine at different times, making for a nice, balanced personality and life. In stressful, uncomfortable situations, the extreme sides of our personalities muscle in and tend to take over. So we end up coming across as painfully shy or REALLY LOUD, and the volume control button slides madly from one end to the other like a naughty poltergeist playing with the sound system in a haunted house. Volume control is one of the main problems we deal with on *WLTM* (see Jeremy's tips on page 112). All the people we've worked with had all the right qualities – it was just a matter of toning them down in some areas and turning them up in others.

Do volume control checks several times during a conversation with someone you're trying to impress to make sure the person you're talking to is getting to meet all the people inside you, not just one. Also remember that alcohol invariably turns up your personality volume. If in doubt, tone everything down (and have a coffee or glass of water while you're at it).

RULE 7:   ONLY APPROACH MEN WHO POINT AT YOU

If he's got his hands on his hips, pointing down toward his genitals, or his thumbs hooked in the waistband or pockets of his trousers, or his hands slid inside his trousers pointing downward, it's likely he's interested. All these gestures mean he's pointing subconsciously to his good bits, willing you to pay attention to him as a mate/male. Other clever me-Tarzan-you-Jane behaviours include standing with his hands on his hips (accentuates his physical size and makes him appear in control) and spreading his legs when seated and tilting his crotch slightly upward to give you a clearer look (no need to get indignant, he's not even aware he's doing it).

RULE 8:   CHECK SHE'S HAVING A GOOD HAIR DAY

Women are always playing with their hair. But what does all that twirling and twisting mean? Here are a few hints.

She's tucking her hair behind her ears: This means business: she's in control and knows what she wants.

She's constantly fiddling with it or obsessively pulling her fingers through it, almost like they're a comb: Not great news here. She's probably restless and unsatisfied, and certainly self-conscious.

She's flicking it around and tossing her head, or perhaps piling it all up, holding it for a second or two, then letting the whole lot drop again: Bingo! This girl's well aware you're watching and letting you have a good look at her face from different angles with different hairstyles. She's confident of how she looks, and also knows you're about to come over. She's got you sussed, so you might as well give in…

She's twisting her hair around her finger: The common perception is that this means she's flirting, but in reality it usually means she's frustrated or bored. She's got long hair and is sucking the ends of it: Not a great look. It also means she's insecure and clingy. Apply only if you don't mind being the surrogate daddy-type of boyfriend.

RULE 9:   IF IN DOUBT, SMILE

The best advice I ever heard about smiling was to smile at others the way you want them to smile at you. Test to see if someone's interested in you by flashing small, quick smiles, catching their eye each time you do so. If they're flashing them back, smile for longer periods and combine with eye contact lasting three or four seconds. Once you're talking face to face, smile with an open mouth as much as possible: part those lips and show your teeth. The more you do, the more flirtatious, open, warm and generous you'll appear. (If you're keeping your lips together because you don't want to expose what's underneath, book into a good cosmetic dentist. Closed-mouth smiles work in the beginning, but once in heavy flirting mode, they destroy any chance of intimacy developing.)

RULE 10:   SEAL THE DEAL WITH A TOUCH

A recent psychology study conducted among students involved touch. When the students returned their library books, the librarian was briefed to 'accidentally' touch some of them on the forearm or hand. Then all the students were asked what they thought of the librarian who served them. In every single case, the people who'd been touched expressed warmer, more positive feelings about her than the students she hadn't made contact with. You don't need to be a university professor to figure the real-life ramifications of all this: if you want someone to think you're fab and remember you, reach out and touch them.

2

Dating Style

Jay Hunt

Having a sense of your own style is terribly important, not just for going on dates but for looking good and feeling confident all the time. Most of us over the age of 25 get stuck in some kind of clothing rut, and it's hard to understand habits, let alone break them, without a bit of help. That's where this section comes in. It's perfectly possible to discover your own personal style: you just need to identify the image you want and learn whether you have the body shape and lifestyle to carry it off successfully.

Clothes and grooming make a statement about who you are – your sexuality, your age, your class – and we all make assumptions about people based on looks. It is not stupid, vain or a waste of time to care about your appearance. And often it's not lack of money or fashion savvy that stops you dressing in the right clothes. It's lack of confidence that prevents you buying what you really want.

Making a change that has a huge visual impact is scary for many people, so the key is to start slowly and build up gradually to more daring choices. It is definitely worth making the effort because if you look good, you are going to be selling yourself better, and the dating world is a tough market-place. Dating style is not about following a set of rigid fashion rules laid down by me. It's about fashion freedom – the way you wear the clothes you have chosen and develop your own personal style.

Some people are taken aback when they realize what their appearance says about them. Indeed, many of *WLTM*'s contributors are surprised at what I tell them about their dummy date appearance. Jon, for example, was amazed that I didn't rate his leather trousers, and Debbie certainly didn't expect to be likened to a poodle-headed barmaid. Some people react defensively to my observations and say, 'Who cares? It's the person inside who counts. We shouldn't be so obsessed with fashion and looks.' The fact is that these people have no idea how to change, and are embarrassed that they need help with something that they secretly feel they should know how to manage. If you are one of these people, you are not alone by any means. The first step to changing for the better is to try answering the following quiz to see how you score on dating style.

What's your dating style?

1. When you look at a photograph of yourself you feel:
   a. Happy it's a great shot.
   b. We all have off days and that was obviously one of yours.
   c. You avoid looking, it would depress you all week.

2. Your wardrobe is:
   a. Disorganized, with more expensive mistakes than you would like to admit.
   b. Colour coordinated and updated pretty well every season.
   c. A war zone crammed with a variety of sizes but nothing in it seems to fit.

3. Dressing to suit your body shape is:
   a. A lottery; how does everyone else seem to manage it?
   b. A bit haphazard; you get there more by luck than judgement.
   c. Easy when you stick to what you know suits you.

4. When you go out socially with your friends you feel:
   a. Generally OK but good-looking people definitely intimidate you.
   b. Confident and flirty, you know you usually look pretty hot.
   c. You hate going out to parties; there's no point anymore, it's too depressing.

5. Your usual outfit for going on a date is:
   a. Something that makes you feel sexy, but you don't really have a fixed rule.
   b. An extreme: either leather, lace or something that screams sex, or you go straight from the office to avoid looking like you have tried too hard.
   c. Something in black for covering up the bad bits.

6. A man who is into facials and personal grooming is:

a. A modern wonder who should be applauded.

b. OK, but only if he doesn't talk about it.

c. A sad joke; stuff like that should be left to the girls.

7. A woman making an effort for a date should:

a. Go for it, with a full evening face on to show that she is interested.

b. Look clean and sexy without too much obvious make-up.

c. Wear more make-up than usual to look glamorous.

8. Going out to buy clothes for yourself is:

a. Only fun if you go with your mates and have a laugh.

b. Great fun but you have to remain focused on your purpose.

c. Something you don't do any more – it's a waste of time.

9. Buying designer-label clothes is:

a. Expensive, but necessary to get people to take you seriously.

b. A waste of money; labels are for suckers.

c. Fun, you like to do it occasionally.

10. When getting ready to go out on a date you take:

a. As much time as you need, it varies.

b. However much time you set aside, there never seems to be enough.

c. No time at all; it's not cool these days to look like you've tried.

11. Your ideal venue for a first date would be:

a. A quiet restaurant you have already checked out.

b. Your local pub so you can get in some drinks with your mates first.

c. A happening bar with atmosphere in case your date is too dull.

12. Your best friend tells you about some amazing new hair product. Do you:

a. Drift off in mid-conversation?

b. Think about how much you hate your hair and wonder if it will work for you?

c. Buy it on your way home; you don't care how much it costs?

13. When buying new scent or aftershave do you:

a. Definitely go by the smell and not the label?
b. Buy only designer smells – you like a power punch for your money?
c. Use the same old one as you have done for years?

14. It is better on a date to be:

a. Underdressed.
b. Overdressed.
c. Haven't a clue.

15. Wearing colour on a date is:

a. Not sexy; black is definitely the way to go.
b. Scary: you sometimes add a bit to your basically black outfit.
c. The quickest way to get a compliment.

16. Wearing no knickers on a date is:

a. A bit of a worry as you would keep needing to check yourself in a
   mirror.
b. Guaranteed to make you feel sexy, and no one need know.
c. Out of the question: you wouldn't dare.

17. Having a new hairstyle is:

a. A nightmare; you have yet to have a haircut that you actually like.
b. Something that is worth planning with a hairdresser you can trust.
c. Something that you have a vague idea about, and think you can
   describe.

18. Looking at fashion magazines is:

a. A good way of seeing new ideas and fashions.
b. A depressing experience all round.
c. Worth a quick flick but you could never look like those models.

19. Your most hated body part is:

a. Your own secret you definitely keep quiet about.
b. Something you will talk about if pressed.
c. Something you make a joke about to others before they mention it.

20. Wearing scuffed shoes on a date is:

    a. To be avoided but no one will notice worn-down heels, will they?

    b. A bad idea that can negate all your other efforts.

    c. No problem. Who's going to notice your feet anyway?

Add up your score.

1.	a. 3,	b. 2,	c. 1
2.	a. 3,	b. 1,	c. 2
3.	a. 1,	b. 2,	c. 3
4.	a. 2,	b. 3,	c. 1
5.	a. 3,	b. 1,	c. 2
6.	a. 3,	b. 2,	c. 1
7.	a. 1,	b. 3,	c. 2
8.	a. 2,	b. 3,	c. 1
9.	a. 2,	b. 1,	c. 3
10.	a. 3,	b. 2,	c. 1
11.	a. 3,	b. 1,	c. 2
12.	a. 1,	b. 2,	c. 3
13.	a. 2,	b. 3,	c. 1
14.	a. 3,	b. 2,	c. 1
15.	a. 1,	b. 2,	c. 3
16.	a. 2,	b. 3,	c. 1
17.	a. 1,	b. 3,	c. 2
18.	a. 3,	b. 1,	c. 2
19.	a. 3,	b. 2,	c. 1
20.	a. 2,	b. 3,	c. 1

If you scored 20–30…

There's quite a bit of work to be done on your dating style. You are probably at one end of the dating style spectrum: either you pull out all the stops (black leather and sexy overkill) or you arrive straight from work, terrified that showing you have made an effort is not cool. Either way, your appearance will not give your date a clue about the real you: to me it suggests that you're probably wanting to be someone else. You have to stop thinking that everyone is better at this game than you. They aren't, but they probably put more work into understanding themselves and their sense of style than you do. You really need to sit down and re-evaluate your personal style. You might think that making an effort is uncool but it most certainly needs to be the first thing you do, as changes are vital before you go out on a date again. Don't be too proud to admit that appearance is important, and stop thinking that caring how you look is a superficial waste of time. You need to start finding fashion fun and learn how to have a laugh about style.

If you scored 31–50...

Personal style is important but you always feel others are doing it better than you. You are interested in fashion but tend to make expensive mistakes when you purchase designer clothes to boost your ego, and although you spend a lot on clothes, you still seem to need a new outfit when you're going on a date. You need to concentrate on doing some work on your body image. What you see in the mirror is probably way out of sync with how others would describe you, and your confidence needs to be worked on before you buy yet more clothes. You've got some hard work ahead to shift old perceptions about style (yours and others') but try not to beat yourself up about fashion mistakes. There are probably a few things on the dating don'ts list that you are guilty of, but everyone makes mistakes, and overall you will probably be forgiven a few faux pas if most other things start to get on track.

If you scored 50–60...

You are definitely on the right track when it comes to date style. Your friends would probably describe you as cool and you have a keen sense of personal style with the confidence to break fashion rules to suit your own needs. You are good at clashing the odd designer label or a fab piece of vintage clothing with high street brands, but you would probably do even better with a bit of a wardrobe update. You need to be aware that dates are not the place to shout about your fashion knowledge; many people find too trendy a date threatening, so make sure you don't end up showing off. The downside of being style conscious is that many people can't or won't keep up, so you must be careful not to dismiss potential dates too soon on the basis that they are not hip enough. Don't judge people too harshly on appearance when it comes to dating. You might need to relax your fashion rules and concentrate on making your date feel comfortable.

Your body type
and how to live with it

Learning to love your body with all its imperfections is a tall order for most people, but there is a way to come to terms with what nature dealt out to you. Most of us have a distorted body image, which doesn't help when it comes to knowing what clothes looks good on us. In all my years of styling I have never met anyone who was completely happy about their body. Celebrities, models, estate agents, engineers... everyone has body parts they would happily swap for something 'better'.

If you too are not 100 per cent satisfied with what your gene pool has handed out, don't just give up. The key to having the 'body beautiful' is knowing how to fake it – big time. Once you have identified what you really don't like, and maybe learnt to like other areas a little bit more, you can get on with the business of dressing your best.

It's not my job to tell people to lose weight or go to the gym five times a week. Chances are it's probably not your body that needs to change but your head. Once you understand and acknowledge your body shape, then you can start to develop a more realistic body image.

Taking responsibility for your body image can be hard, especially if you have spent your life making excuses. A lot of people let partners pick clothes for them, can't make decisions without the approval of their best friend, or blame their job for the fact that they have to dress a certain way. Jon, one of the contributors on *WLTM*, had made the classic mistake of putting his life on hold until he met his one true love. This included not buying clothes because he longed for someone else to take that responsibility. Don't make this mistake.

There are many ways of avoiding responsibility for making yourself look good, but you can't avoid it for ever. *You* have to decide on your personal style, not use someone or something else as a scapegoat for hating your image.

The roots of body image, good or bad, often lie in childhood. We all remember the torture of playground taunts, which can create insecurities that take years to shift. I was the fat one in the class, and until recently could only see that overweight child looking back at me in the mirror. *WLTM* guest Richard admitted to me that he had been a late developer and was always the smallest in the class, which led him to describe himself as a 'twiglet' at any opportunity. Children pick on anyone different – the thinnest, the tallest, the one who wears glasses, the one with a birthmark, the early or late developer... Teasing is cruel, but it happens, and it can be hard to shift your perceptions, even if you've now lost weight, wear contact lenses, or whatever. Your brain still registers an out-of-date, negative body image.

As adults there are plenty of mental tricks going on when it comes to body image, and they can come in useful to avoid doing the homework I set in this chapter. However, if you want to learn how to look good, you have to take an honest look at your body, accept it and decide to like the way you are today.

Let's be honest here: is it really worth putting important desires on hold, such as finding a partner, until you are fatter, thinner, have had your breasts done, or can afford hair replacement therapy? Everyone has insecurities about their bodies, but perspective is the key.

It is time to realize that the way you see yourself is probably very different from how others see you, and the following exercise should boost your body confidence.

Reassessing your body image

You need to start seeing yourself as others do. When you look at a photograph or video of yourself, you are seeing yourself as others do, and that can be a shock. But rather than resorting to a crash diet or moving into the gym, you need to gain perspective on the different parts of your body: don't see the whole thing as negative.

STAND IN FRONT OF A FULL-LENGTH MIRROR AND LOOK AT EACH BODY PART

Think how it has changed over the years. Then mark yourself out of 10 (zero being the lowest, no negative points allowed) for each body part based on what it looks like today.

Hair You might hate your current style, but is it glossy or a great colour?

Eyes Could you make more of them? Is it the bushy eyebrows that you really hate?

Skin Would you like it more if you knew how to look after it?

Lips and smile Would a visit to the dentist make a difference?

Shoulders and back Could they look good if you worked on your posture?

Arms Is it all of them or just the upper parts you loathe?

HOMEWORK:

HOW BAD IS YOUR BODY IMAGE?

Don't be alarmed if this homework makes you feel insecure. You've spent years pretending you don't care, so it might be scary to admit that you do. Get a friend to do the exercises too and compare notes afterwards. It can help to have another person's perspective on your answers.

Ask yourself the following questions:
1. Do you go out of your way to avoid looking in a full-length mirror?
2. Do you want to look away when you see photographs of yourself or watch yourself on a home video camera?
3. Do you dislike going clothes shopping?
4. Do you avoid new styles of clothes, thinking they are 'not for you'?
5. Do you always end up in black?
6. Do you wish that the way you look didn't matter?
7. Do you find yourself always copying someone else's style?
8. Do you think everyone else is better looking than you are?
9. Do you often make jokes about your appearance to others?
10. Do you always think you could look better?

If you answered yes to more than four of these questions, there is some serious work to be done with your head. Read on – the answers are all here.

Chest Would it be a lot better if you dressed in clothes that suit you?

Stomach Is it really that big? Is the lower or upper part much flatter than the rest?

Legs and thighs You might hate your thighs, but have you got good ankles?

Bum We all ask if it looks too big, but is it in proportion to the rest of you?

Check your results. The lower the numbers, the worse your body image, but don't worry if there are no high marks. There should be a pattern. Even if you've given your legs and thighs just one out of 10, your hair three, and your skin two, you should be able to start judging which areas you like more than others.

WLTM contributor Louise found it very difficult to do this exercise as it brought back painful feelings about how she had always been teased for having thin hair. Nonetheless, it did motivate her to explore what she could do about it, and it also finally made her realize that she possessed a pair of fabulous legs.

Once you know your hate areas and the parts you don't exactly love but don't mind, you are ready for the next stage. This is the fun part, as you begin to absorb the most important lesson of body image: how to minimize your hate list and maximize your like list by using clothes to fake perfection.

Faking the perfect body

I don't believe in sticking to rigid clothing rules when it comes to style and colour, but there are certain tricks that deceive the eye and turn you into a clothing con artist when it comes to disguising the most common body problems.

MEN

The problems that men most often complain about are to do with height, hair and general build. In every instance there's always a quick fix.

If you think you're too short...

Don't wear shoes with a built-in lift, or high cowboy boots – they don't make you look taller, just stupid; don't wear your trousers too short or add massive turn-ups.

Do wear sleeves and trousers as long as you can without them looking too big for you: it can add an extra inch to your height. Do go for vertical patterns, stripes, single-breasted jackets, straight-leg trousers or jeans, and narrow ties.

If you think you're too tall...

Don't wear jackets done right up; avoid jackets with zips down the front, and don't wear the same colour from head to toe. Avoid pinstripe suits, vertical patterns, jackets that end at the waist, and very thin ties.

Do wear longer jackets, double-breasted suits and trousers with a low waist. Try lower-cut jeans in dark denim, layering different length tops and jackets.

If you think you're too bulky...

Don't wear tops or jackets with extra padding; avoid doing shirts right up and don't sport loud ties. Buy your correct neck size (or half an inch bigger) in formal shirts, and never wear a small watch on a pudgy wrist. Avoid bulky jumpers or cable knits, and forget about polo-neck sweaters. Don't wear trousers made of stiff fabric or with turn-ups.

Do wear V-necks, jumpers or shirts with a vertical pattern, shirts with narrow or open collars, ties in a single discreet colour, subtle pinstripes, and high-fastening jackets with three or even four buttons. Choose close-fitting, lightweight tops in dark colours, fine knitwear that skims rather than swamps the body, and wear relaxed-fit jeans.

If you think you're too weedy...

Don't wear V-necked shirts or jumpers. Avoid narrow ties, vertical stripes, pinstriped suits, shiny fabrics, or very tight-fitting tops that hug your shoulders.

Do wear padded jackets and waistcoats over T-shirts, and choose checked suits and double-breasted jackets. Wear baggy, low-slung combat trousers à la David Beckham, cargo pants with pockets on the sides, horizontal details on tops, bulky knit sweaters and polo necks, and button shirts up to the max.

If you think you have a big stomach...

Don't wear waistcoats or anything too small: it will strain across a larger stomach. Avoid man-made fibres that develop static and cling to a bulge. Don't wear trousers over your stomach à la Simon Cowell: it looks ridiculous. Avoid double-breasted jackets, shiny fabrics and light colours.

Do wear loose-fitting cotton or linen clothes in dark shades. Buy trousers big enough to do up on (rather than under) the stomach. Make sure ties are wide and meet your waistband. Wear trousers and jacket in the same colour, and go for single-breasted jackets every time.

If you think you have a large bum...

Don't wear trousers in camel, white or bleached denim, and avoid jeans with fussy details. Avoid low-cut trousers that reveal any hint of builder's bum when you bend over, and don't wear shiny fabrics.

Do wear dark colours on your lower half. Choose trousers in plain, non-shiny fabric, loose or baggy fit jeans with minimal detailing, and no underwear poking out.

If you think you have small feet...

Don't go for intricate patterns or small stitching; footwear needs to be bold. Loafers will just look silly.

Do butch up your feet. Go for thick soles, big round toes, motorcycle boots or sturdy dark lace-ups with jeans.

If you think you have big feet...

Don't go for light-coloured leather, fussy details or tassels. Avoid white-based trainers and bright stripes.

Do go for dark leather, the plainer the better; choose black loafers and black or dark grey trainers with discreet trims.

WOMEN

I've yet to meet a woman in the world who doesn't think she's too fat. Apart from their obsession with weight, most women have the same hang-ups as men.

If you think you're too short...

Don't wear clothes with horizontal details or stripes; don't go in for layering; don't wear too many colours at once; avoid big accessories and don't wear too many; don't wear bags slung across the body; avoid trousers with turn-ups or very wide legs; don't buy trousers that are too long and shorten them – it will alter the fit and not for the better; say no to short A-line skirts or large prints.

Do wear outfits in one colour and slim-fitting straight-leg trousers; look leggier by wearing skirts, tights and shoes in the same tones; wear simple lines and keep to small accessories. Do scour shops for petite ranges of clothes, and don't be too embarrassed to look in the teenage girls' section; wear one-button jackets done up above the waistline to fake height.

If you think you're too tall...

Don't wear clothes with vertical lines or patterns, or pinstripe suits; avoid wearing one colour from head to toe; don't wear crop tops or very small jewellery, and don't carry tiny girlie handbags.

Do wear low kitten heels rather than completely flat shoes; try layering, and skirts with a frilled or patterned hem; wear low-waisted bootcut or straight-leg trousers and jeans; don't be afraid to carry big handbags or ones you can sling across your body.

If you think your breasts are too big...

Don't wear too small a bra and spill over the front, back and sides. Ignore tops in pastel shades, with ruffles or thin spaghetti straps, delicate camisole tops and complicated necklines. Avoid bulky sweaters, necklines that are too revealing, tops in spangly fabrics, droopy shoulders and sloppy T-shirts, and watch out for any hint of pulling on shirts.

Do wear tailored shirts and subtle V-neck tops that hint at some cleavage rather than showing off the lot; wear dark colours in matt fabrics on the upper half. Wear a bra that fits, no matter what size it says on the label; choose wide-leg or bootleg trousers, or fuller skirts to balance your heavier top half. Try scooped necklines in plain fabrics.

If you think your breasts are too small...

Don't assume any old bra with a bit of padding will make you look better; it must fit so make sure that seams and padding can't be seen through your top. Avoid going bra-less under flimsy fabrics: nipples a go-go should be left to the bedroom.

Do wear a necklace that draws attention to the chest area as a whole rather than to your cup size. Halterneck tops give width to narrow shoulders. Wear pretty tops or dresses with spaghetti straps to show off attractive shoulders and arms. Go for curvy jackets nipped in at the waist, tops in paler colours than your bottom half, coat-dresses and ballet-style wrapover cardigans.

If you think your hips and thighs are too big...

Don't wear bias-cut skirts or dresses that cling, narrow-leg trousers or jeans, or flat shoes. Say no to any kind of cropped top and tapered knee-length skirts. Avoid cargo pants, combats with side pockets, and belted jackets or coats that flare out over the hips. Don't wear belts that cinch the waist.

Do wear bootleg or flare-cut dark denim jeans in stretch fabric for a relaxed line over curves. Team them with heels, low-slung belts and fine-knit cardigans with just the top button done up. Baggy cotton trousers or parachute trousers à la All Saints are a casual alternative. Wear a close-fitting denim skirt to below the knee. Knee-length jackets with structured shoulders will balance out a heavier bottom half. Get a tailor to take out the pockets in trousers or sew them shut to flatten the area.

If you think your bottom is too big…

Don't wear light-coloured fabric below your waist. Avoid narrow legs, shiny fabric or leather trousers. Don't wear thin heels – they make you look like you could topple over. Avoid oversized trousers or jeans (it's too obvious), jeans with detailing and pockets, short skirts, anything half a size too small, and bias-cut dresses that hug the bum.

Do wear looser-fit, lower-slung trousers that skim over your bum, and longer length jackets that end below your bottom in a simple, single-breasted style. Team them with open-toe shoes. Wear dark colours on your bottom half; jeans in dark stretch denim will minimize baggy waist problems. Choose pinstripe trousers and those with no back pockets. Try tying a fine-knit cardigan around your waist for casual camouflage.

If you think your stomach is too big…

Don't wear skirts or dresses in flimsy fabrics that offer no support, drawstring waist trousers or low-cut hipsters, elastic-waisted tops, big prints or tiny floral prints. Don't wear support knickers that are too small or tops that contain Lycra (they will just emphasize a spare tyre), and avoid tops designed to be tucked in.

Do wear denim skirts with a zip or buttons at the front – the fabric is strong enough to hold your stomach in. Choose shirts or cardigans with buttons and leave the last three or four undone to skim over the tummy. Wear longer length jackets, trousers that zip at the side, flat-fronted skirts with low-slung waistbands, and big chunky belts slung around the lower stomach. Long and lean stretch jeans help to elongate the body.

If you think your legs and ankles are too chunky…

Don't wear mini-skirts, calf-length skirts or boots, or light-coloured or shiny tights. Don't let your hem fall at the fattest part of your leg. Avoid delicate strappy shoes, ankle straps or ankle chains. Don't wear heels above 2.5 inches if you are a size four or under – you will just look off balance,

Do wear skirts that end just below the knee to make lower legs look longer. Wear wedges, low-cut shoes, or black knee-length boots in suede or stretch fabric if they won't do up around calves. Wear dark-coloured plain tights in winter and fake tan in summer; sandals with broad straps across the foot help to disguise puffy ankles.

Now you understand how to fake your look, it's time to see how much of your existing wardrobe is going to help rather than hinder you as a master/mistress of disguise.

How to get your wardobe working for you

Most of us do not use our wardrobes for the purpose for which they were designed. I have lost count of the times I have arrived at clients' houses to find their wardrobe being used for storing old school reports, board games, tins of paint, torn sheets: it seems any old junk gets thrown in with their clothes. No wonder they hated opening their wardrobe doors.

Set aside half a day for a wardrobe clear-out and have some black bin bags at the ready. Having someone to help you is also a good idea as you might find it harder than you think to get rid of some of the garments lurking in your wardrobe. You will undoubtedly come across quite a few 'security blanket' items – the jumper your mother gave you for Christmas seven years ago, a scarf or tie an ex bought you on a romantic weekend in Venice, the old leather jacket from your racy student days… Somehow there is always a reason why you can't throw certain clothes away. Most of us are secret clothes hoarders, and yet I don't think I have ever met anyone who has not at some point stood in front of a stuffed wardrobe and wailed that they have nothing suitable to wear. Most of us, if we're honest, have a much bigger percentage of things we don't wear in our wardrobe than things we actually do. We tend to wear about 20 per cent of what's in our wardrobes, which means that there is an awful lot of useless clobber to sift through and throw away.

Many of my clients find going through their wardrobe a difficult process: they say it makes them feel really exposed. When Jo from *WLTM* did a wardrobe clear-out she was amazed to discover how many times she had bought the same item in different colours. It certainly explained why she was so bored with her clothes.

There's no doubt that having a clear-out can be tough, especially doing it on your own, which is why I suggest that you ask a really good friend to come over and help. This will keep you on track and clearing out rather than reminiscing over every item and then putting everything back in again. Please do not ask your partner or your mother to help you with this activity. You need to pick a friend who is going to be really objective and honest, as you are about to let your purchasing history in all its uneconomic reality hit you in the face.

Do remember, this is a time to be totally focused on moving forward. Think of your clear-out as a positive experience and a simplifying exercise. I promise you that no one I have ever done this with has phoned me afterwards to express regret, no matter how painful and difficult they found the process at the time.

First, you need to realize that many of the items in your wardrobe are there for different reasons. The most common are:

- They don't fit because you are now fatter.
- They don't fit because you are now thinner.
- They remind you of an ex-lover or a different time in your life.
- They were given to you by relatives or exes and you feel guilty about getting rid of them.
- They just don't suit you.
- They were so expensive that you feel you have to keep them.

STEP 1: Prepare yourself

Make sure you are wearing clothes that are easy to put on and take off as you are going to be doing a lot of trying on.

STEP 2: Empty the wardrobe

Take all your clothes out of the wardrobe and pile them up on your bed. Remove all the hangers and throw away any that are broken or out of shape. Wire hangers are never a good idea – they bend, things fall off them, they don't help clothes to keep their shape… It really is worth buying some wooden hangers, even if you use them only for your more expensive items.

STEP 3: Divide and rule

Spread your clothes on the bed so you can see what you are doing and start to sift. You are aiming to create three new piles:

- Clothes to keep.
- Clothes that are maybes.
- Clothes to sell or give to charity shops.

Try not to get sidetracked. If you are taking too long deciding over one item, put it on the maybe pile. But do beware: this is the pile that is easiest to go for, so limit it to just 10 items. You must be tough or your wardrobe clear-out will come to nothing.

STEP 4 : How to decide what has to go

Many clients fear that I am going to make them throw everything away and worry about the cost of starting again. I may be ruthless but I'm not stupid. We all need to keep some of our clothes, even if we want to restock from scratch.

We all get used to seeing our wardrobes packed full of clothes, and it is reassuring in a way. It's a bit like the comfort you feel when your fridge is fully stocked. But we clear the fridge of things past their sell-by dates every week, and restock regularly. Your wardrobe needs that basic approach.

I would be lying if I didn't admit that you will probably end up with fewer clothes than you've ever had in your wardrobe. But look at it this way: you will never again end up with so much unused clutter that has cost you money. Don't forget that this is an exercise in moving forward, and don't be surprised if you start to feel uncomfortable or insecure: that's perfectly normal.

Put on an item of clothing from your wardrobe and if it fits into one of the following four categories, put it on the pile to throw out.

- You haven't worn it for over a year.
- It's worn out.
- It doesn't fit.
- You just don't feel good in it, but it was expensive.

If you buy a winter coat and don't wear it, promising yourself that next winter it really will come into its own, take it from me – it won't. In my experience, if you buy clothes and wear them as soon as you get them home, you generally find they are winners. Clothes that stay in the bag or go straight to the back of the wardrobe rarely see the light of day again. If you love something and it works, you might wear it for years. If it's hanging about waiting for the right time, it's never going to happen. Throw it.

A lot of people say, 'Oh, but it's a classic, and classics never go out of style.' This is one big fashion myth. Even if the same classic style comes back, it's never quite the same. It might have wider lapels, puffed sleeves, no belt, but always something that your item of clothing misses yet again. Buying classic and getting it to work for ever is what fashion editors do. No one else gets it quite right, so don't feel bad if you don't – you're not alone.

Worn-out clothes are never sexy. Look out for the most common offenders: clothes that have lost their shape through too much wear, bobbled fabrics that are past being razored, black clothes that are now grey, trousers that are worn on the inner thigh, shoes that have seen better days. Put all these in the throwing-out pile now. The only exceptions to this rule are, if you have any, cashmere jumpers because these can still look good for casual wear no matter how battered they are. Remember, you can never make a worn-out item look smart.

Clothes that don't fit must not stay in the wardrobe. Most of us have weight fluctuations one way or the other, and keeping clothes that no longer fit is a big mistake. Many people lose weight and hang on to their old 'fat clothes' just in case they pile it on again. If you've managed to lose weight, have the confidence to say goodbye to those bigger sizes. Even if you do end up putting weight on again, you will not want to wear those clothes as they will remind you of an 'old you', which for most people is not a positive thing. Very rare indeed is the person who is truly happy being bigger. Sue, one of the guests on *WLTM*, found she had about 16 different lifestyles within her wardrobe and ended up throwing away more than she ever thought she had. The throw-away rule applies to all those things you wore 10 years ago when you were three sizes smaller and dream of wearing again. They are a negative reminder of times past and probably make you feel bad every time you clap eyes on them, so enjoy saying goodbye. Other offenders are items of clothing you have bought to 'slim into', but you've never quite got round to losing the half a stone that will let you do the trousers up, or lost the bulge that appears over the top. You have to bite the bullet and start buying clothes for the size that you are today, not the size that you want to be in your dreams.

Spending lots on an item does not guarantee that it will be a success, and such mistakes really bring home just how much money you've wasted over the years. Confronting how much you have frittered away on the right label but the wrong look is tough, but it must be done. Put articles in this category on the throw-away pile, and think about taking them to a second-hand shop that will sell them for you in return for a percentage. Even a small amount for your old clothes is better than nothing, certainly preferable to seeing them every time you open the wardrobe. These guilty purchases are not good for your self-esteem, but cheer yourself by accepting that this exercise will help you to avoid making the same mistakes again.

STEP 5: How to decide what to keep

Put the item of clothing on and ask yourself the following questions:
- Do I still like it?
- Do I feel good/sexy in it?
- Does it still fit?
- Does it go with other things?

There will probably not be too many items that get a yes to all of the above, but if the answer is yes to a few, they can definitely go back in your new, pared-down wardrobe. For a lot of people these items will be black. Others might hang on to, say, a business suit that makes them feel in control, or a pair of jeans that they think makes their bum look good.

Make a note of the things that get the ticks so that you can start to identify what you really like wearing. This will help you to build your new wardrobe with other feel-good items. Remember the feeling when you put on your favourite clothes. You probably can't quite understand why one jacket more than another makes you feel sexy, gets more compliments than other more expensive jackets, but whatever it is, that is the feeling you want to have from items in your new wardrobe, and that's the feeling new additions should provoke too.

STEP 6: Imposing order

Once you have decided what to keep, put your clothes back in a way that is easy to maintain – longer items at one end, shorter at the other. Then group similar items together – shirts, tops, trousers, – and arrange them according to colour to make them easier to find. Don't overstuff your wardrobe: you should be able to move the hangers around, as you can in shops. If you need brute force to extract a shirt, there is too much in there. Use a chest of drawers for T-shirts and casual tops to let your wardrobe have a bit of space. Give priority space to things you need. (*WLTM* contributor Jon kept his underwear in a shoebox by his bed and had an empty chest of drawers in his room – until I got in there!) Hang up scarves and ties (undo any knots first) and they will last better. Shoes keep their shape with shoe trees, but I have only ever met one person who does this with every pair. Do like the rest of us and buy just a couple of pairs for your favourite designer shoes.

Underwear, socks, tights, bags, jewellery and cufflinks all need to be gone through. Bras that don't fit, shapeless grey pants, the designer thong that you can't stand for more than 10 minutes – all go in the bin. So do the single gloves, the cufflinks that don't fasten properly and the bag with the broken handle. Be brutal: the only things that get to stay are the ones that make you feel great.

The good news is that there should now be some room in your wardrobe for new purchases. All that effort surely deserves some reward…

POST CLEAR-OUT TIPS
- Buy some lavender sachets or cedar-scented balls to hang in the wardrobe. They make things smell better and are good moth deterrents.
- Build up a collection of decent hangers: they do make a difference. If you must use wire hangers for your clothes, you can make them work more efficiently by wrapping elastic bands about 2 inches from each end. This will prevent smaller items or light fabrics from slipping off.
- Think before chucking shoes. Re-heeling might give them a new lease of life.

HOMEWORK:

BUILD ON YOUR SUCCESS

Clearing out your wardrobe is a cathartic exercise, but there is yet more to do to help you get to grips with your clothes. You are aiming to build up a wardrobe that works for you, but you must be realistic about your lifestyle. You hear a lot of talk about 'capsule' wardrobes these days, clothes to take you from the office to cocktails to dinner, etc., but for most people life is not that simple.

- Work out what clothes you wear the most and why, and get a friend to help you identify the gaps in your wardrobe. Do you really need more work clothes or is it casual outfits that would pull your wardrobe together? *WLTM* contributor Richard had a whole wardrobe full of clothes that I told him would suit a retired chairman of the Rotary Club. They were clothes he liked and that his parents approved of, but they were for a lifestyle he didn't have. He desperately needed more casual clothes to make him look less prissy, more his age, so the content of his wardrobe shifted dramatically.
- Are your accessories up to date or just an uncoordinated mess? Note the things that you actually need for your lifestyle, not the clothes you think you need for a lifestyle you dream of.
- Write a list of your needs from the inside out – underwear to overcoats – and make a separate list for shoes and accessories.

Shopping

Forget how you used to shop, forget how much you hated your local high street, forget the money you have wasted in the past. Your next shopping trip is going to be a surefire winner, but there are a few things you can do to help yourself before you leave the house.

Consult the glossies

At the end of the last section your homework was to make a list of the gaps in your wardrobe. With that in mind, get a whole bunch of fashion magazines and tear out pictures of any outfits that you like. Don't worry if the complete outfit is not ideal: perhaps you like just the collar of a jacket, or the heel on a shoe. The important thing is to get flicking and tearing.

When you have a pile of about 20–30 sheets, look through them and a pattern will begin to emerge. You may have to do this a couple of times, so start about a week before you plan to go shopping. Don't do it in bed the night before.

You should be starting to spot that you have a weakness for kitten heels, pinstripe suits, pink accessories, spotty ties, whatever turns you on. This new-found knowledge will help you define your list of needs before you hit the high street. (If in doubt that some of the things you like might not suit you, see the style advice on pages 55–9.)

WLTM contributor Jo found that analysing what her favourite celebrity icons were wearing and why helped her to develop her own sense of style. She was a huge fan of Sarah Jessica Parker (*Sex and the City*) but at first could not see how to adapt a celebrity style to herself. By using magazines to analyze the look and see how items were put together, and how small things could be used by Jo to personalize an outfit, she found a way to create her own celebrity-inspired style.

Don't get depressed by shots of models and celebrities looking fabulous in their designer outfits. You should be savvy enough by now to know that these images are styled to perfection, and even top models are airbrushed to within an inch of their lives. The aim of this section is to help you shape and build your own style, not to have you comparing yourself with others.

Hone your list

Your wardrobe homework will have helped you to identify the gaps in your wardrobe, so now write a list of the most important items you are lacking, plus other key items that would pull existing outfits together. You should also be able to identify what item(s) you tend to waste money on and overbuy. One client who did this exercise realized that she had 18 pairs of black trousers in her wardrobe, while a businessman I know had 24 practically identical white shirts. This comfort overbuying is not going to happen again.

YOUR LIST SHOULD HAVE ON IT:
- How much you want to spend that day.
- What you actually want – jacket, shoes, trousers, etc.
- What items of clothing you already own that the new item will go with.

Once you have this list, it's easy to consult it when out shopping and keep focused on what you need. Budgets are made for a reason, but I won't deny that many of my best purchases were made when I got that adrenaline rush from spending just a bit more than I should. Our minds can play fantastic tricks in shops, convincing us that the most unsuitable item should be bought, but we then crash back to reality on getting home. Your list will help stop high street flights of fancy.

Another advantage of having a list is that it stops you vaguely searching for some unspecified item that you're convinced will miraculously change your whole life. I call this fantasy shopping and it generally results in a feeling of failure. This takes three forms, with which you may be familiar: 1.) You go home empty-handed because you couldn't find this dream garment, which reinforces how much you hate shopping. 2.) You buy something fantastically expensive because you convince yourself that it fulfils your fantasy. 3.) You make a desperate purchase, usually of something you already have in abundance, because it's better than going home with nothing.

Keep your list to hand and make a note on it of the shops you are going to target.

Where should you go shopping?

Note down the labels of the clothes left in your wardrobe and there will probably be one or two labels that predominate. Put two shops that sell these labels at the top of your list. In addition, you are going to try two new shops every time you go out so that you eventually end up with a core of about four shops that work for you: these have styles you like and the clothes fit.

Good shoppers know what stores have clothes that are cut to suit them, where the longer length trousers are always long enough, and where the expensive buttons and trimmings that get noticed. There is no shortcut to accumulating this knowledge for yourself apart from going into shops and trying things on. Set yourself about an hour in total to visit two new shops, and don't forget to revisit shops that you may feel are too young, too old or too trendy. High street shops are constantly evolving, so don't write anywhere off without trying it first.

WLTM contributor Richard didn't know where to start when he hit the high street on his own, having previously done all his shopping with his parents in department stores. By trial and error, he researched shops that catered for his age group and became much more confident in his choices. Be prepared when you start this process to make the odd mistake, and include some cheaper shops in your research. Don't forget to check the returns policy. Most high street shops will give refunds on items in perfect condition if returned within 14–28 days. Keep the receipts and at the end of the week remind yourself of how many times you have worn your new item. In my experience, if you haven't worn it within the first two weeks of purchase, you won't ever wear it, so take it back.

The British high street is one of the best in the world for affordable, up-to-date merchandise, so make the most of it.

SHOPPING TIPS
- Don't confuse style with money. You can't buy someone else's style – you have to work at finding your own.
- Set yourself a time limit to go shopping so that you don't spend all day getting frustrated.
- Shopping is exhausting, so wear comfy shoes, clothes that you can slip on and off easily, and take plenty of coffee stops.
- Don't have preconceived ideas about shops if you have not been in any for a while. Images change, so don't dismiss them too quickly.
- Try new places to shop. Going to another town could prevent you from falling into your usual pattern of shopping.

How to make a good purchase

Stick to buying what you have gone out for, and consult your list to check your requirements before you purchase. This can be harder than you think because you are bound to see the most fantastic pair of shoes when you are busy shopping for a sensible black jacket. If you do, fine, but put them on hold. When you get home, consult your shoe list. If the shoes still seem a good idea, go back and get them. In the early days, when you are building up confidence at shopping, do try to concentrate on buying one item at a time and take just the relevant list with you.

Don't be seduced by labels

Buying famous labels is no substitute for acquiring fashion confidence. It's fun and can be quite affordable to buy designer sunglasses, jeans or trainers, but when it comes to other items, you can be talking very serious money. Some people think the answer to looking good is spending lots of money. Not true. Wearing top-to-toe designer labels is a huge statement, and if you buy something because of the label rather than because you like it, it's a mistake. You must get to grips with the fact that a logo is not a replacement for self-confidence.

COLOUR GUIDELINES
- Black does not suit everybody. Try using navy, khaki or grey as a base instead.
- Treat denim as you would black: it is a neutral colour and goes with everything.
- Mix colour with colour instead of with black. Look at people in the street and in magazines to see what colours they combine successfully if you feel nervous about attempting this.
- Most people look awful in acidic colours, such as lime green.
- If a colour doesn't suit your face, you can still wear it below the waist.

Don't be a fashion victim

It's not difficult to look trendy. You just go and buy the look of the season, which most of the high street stores will have knocked off pretty quickly. However, it does tend to look stupid when you buy things because they are 'in' rather than because they suit you. Clever shoppers update with accessories, buying a new bag, trainers, sunglasses or whatever to make their look seem more current. This is less expensive and less risky than buying whole outfits. Stick to buying 'now' purchases at cheaper shops. If they turn out to be one-season wonders, you won't feel too guilty about throwing them away when the fashion has passed.

If you're tempted by more than one 'now' item, just remember how many fashion victims are on the nation's list of sexiest personalities – not many.

Don't get obsessed by colour

I don't have much time for the complicated rulings these days about colours. Who wants to be categorized for ever as a winter or spring person with a list of rigid colour rules? It seems that some people have made an awful lot of money out of a bit of common sense. Don't be afraid of experimenting with colour, but do try it on before you say it does or doesn't suit you. Everyone thinks putting colours together is tricky, but it's easy if you trust your instinct and use common sense.

Before you buy

You've made your selection(s) but before you pay, ask yourself the following questions:
- Do I really like it? (Don't buy it just because the shop assistant says it looks good.)
- Is it worth the money?
- Do I feel really good in it?
- Do I want to wear it now?
- If it's for a date, do I feel sexy in it?

If you answer yes to four of these questions, go ahead and buy.

HOMEWORK:
STOP BEFORE YOU START

Don't be one of those people who end up at the cash desk without quite realizing how they got there.
- Do your research before you go out, checking through your collection of fashion cuttings to remind yourself what you really want.
- Do ask people you meet where they bought something if it catches your eye.
- Do look around at how other people put colour and looks together.
- Do browse the Internet's numerous fashion sites to see what's coming up and what's looking good.

Grooming and make-up

Now you've got your outfit right, don't get thrown off course by having the wrong hairstyle. The colour and style of your hair are a badge of identity: they should fit in with your image, not detract from it or dictate it. Unfortunately, it is all too easy to get it wrong, as I told Debbie and her poodle perm on *WLTM*.

HAIR TRUTHS
- Hair can create a bigger first impression than face or clothes.
- Everyone wants the hair they don't have.
- A hairdresser can only change your look, not your life.
- Spur of the moment haircuts rarely make you happy.
- Not everyone suits being blonde.
- Your hair will look fantastic the day you get it cut.
- A comb-over never fools anyone: stubble is a better look if you're suffering from lack of hair.
- Straight hair always looks shinier than curly hair.
- Don't have a high-maintenance haircut if you don't even own a hairdryer.
- Home bleaching is rarely successful.

When you are going for a new haircut or colour, do go to the most experienced hairdresser you can. It will be expensive, but you can save money later by going to your local salon for trims or re-colouring. It is easy for a less experienced hairdresser to follow the shape or colour put in by a real expert, and the upkeep will be less.

When you get to the salon

There's no doubt about it: hairdressers are powerful people. They can change your image with one snip of their scissors, but remember that it's in their interest to make you happy and have you look good on leaving the salon. Start by having a full and frank discussion with the hairdresser. Stand up to show your proportions and ask for advice about the sort of cut that suits your body shape. Hair shots in magazines tend to be heavily styled, so listen to what the hairdresser says is achievable with your type of hair. There are all sorts of products to add volume, straighten or curl hair. The aim is to make the most of what you've got.

Don't be afraid to show the hairdresser photos of the styles you like. This will give a clearer idea of what you're after, but do be realistic. You might be able to have hair like Meg Ryan or Brad Pitt, but don't expect to leave the salon with their face or bank balance. Photos can also be used to show the colour and length you want. They are more reliable than pointing and describing.

If you're going from long hair to short, don't be afraid to ask the hairdresser to cut off the length in stages so you can decide what you like. Remember, you're in control. If you're changing the colour, however, the hairdresser really will know best: too light and you look washed out, too dark and your features lose definition. A good rule of thumb is to keep within three shades of your natural colour.

Most people look great when they come out of the hairdresser's, but will they continue to look good when they do it themselves? Ask how easy the style is to recreate at home before you decide to have it. If it takes more than a hairdryer and longer than 10 minutes to do yourself, do you really want it?

Choosing a style

Your face shape and hair type will dictate how many miracles a hairdresser can manage, so consider the following when deciding on a new style.

ROUND FACE (AS WIDE AS IT IS LONG)
(Martine McCutcheon, Cameron Diaz, Matthew Perry, Lenny Henry)
Women should avoid blunt and heavy styles, and one-length fringes. Go for a layered cut around the face or on the shoulder. Avoid severe bobs or big curly hair. A longer length helps to give the face a slimmer appearance.
Men need a cut with straight lines to create balance. Closely tapered hair at the sides with length on top creates a more square shape.

SQUARE FACE (JAW AS WIDE AS FOREHEAD)
(Sophie Ellis Bextor, Minnie Driver, Brad Pitt, Hugh Grant)
Women with this face shape can look masculine with a short haircut, so soften the face with hair falling below the chin. Try longer length grown-out crops or layered bobs with wisps around the face, and off-centre partings. Avoid slicked-back hair.
Men should avoid a square cut. Leave the hair longer on top and full at the sides. Stick to medium-length sideburns for balance.

LONG FACE (LONGER THAN IT IS WIDE)

(Sarah Jessica Parker, Gwyneth Paltrow, Jamie Theakston, Noah Wyle)

Women should aim for added fullness and a fringe to shorten the face. Never go shorter than chin length. Avoid height on the crown, but if pinning hair up, try to add volume at the sides.

Men need to widen and shorten the forehead, so go short, cut close at the ears and on top of the head. Avoid puffy styles. Add the volume at the sides, not on top, and don't opt for a centre parting.

HEART-SHAPED FACE (WIDEST AT THE FOREHEAD)

(Helena Christenson, Sophie Dahl, Graham Norton, Jude Law)

Women need to balance the forehead, so go for long layered fringes, or a bob that kicks out at chin level.

Men should go flat at the sides and ruffled on top. Keep hair around the side of the face straight if possible, and try growing heavy stubble to balance out the upper and lower parts of the face.

OVAL FACE (ONE AND HALF TIMES AS LONG AS IT IS WIDE)

(Naomi Campbell, Kate Moss, Tom Cruise, David Beckham)

Women can take a variety of looks because this face shape is balanced. Feel free to experiment which whatever takes your fancy.

Men also have more flexibility: the hair can take any parting, be worn back from the face or combed forward – you can't really go wrong.

Body beautiful

Your hair may be your crowning glory, but it doesn't pay to ignore or neglect the other parts of your face and body. Here are some quick maintenance reminders.

SKIN

As everyone knows these days, skin needs to be clear and clean to look good. Men have finally realized it is sensible to look after their skin – it's not just girlie nonsense. If you are worried about oily skin on your date, do invest in some mattifying lotion. Shungu, one of our *WLTM* contributors, was really self-conscious about her oily skin and felt everyone noticed it. When she got hold of some mattifying lotion it improved her self-confidence before the evening 100 per cent. It is clear and odourless and will keep shine at bay, especially when you're under stress. If you have a receding hairline, don't forget to rub it on there too: shiny bald plates are not sexy.

Most of us look and feel better with a bit of a tan, but if you're feeling pasty, don't head off for a sunbed treatment – they're not a healthy option. Just apply a bit of fake tan. There is a huge range of mousses, lotions and sprays that are totally different from the strong-smelling, streaky orange nightmares we all remember. The trick of successful self-tanning is to exfoliate and moisturize beforehand, rubbing extra cream into particularly dry areas, such as knees, heels and elbows. Apply the tanning lotion only to those parts that normally see the sun (not the soles of your feet, for example). Wash your hands thoroughly when you've finished or the whole world will know the secret of your healthy glow.

TO SHAVE OR NOT TO SHAVE?

Clean shaven, stubble or bearded? The choice is yours, but do be aware that most women don't like excessive facial hair.

Don't shave just before a date: it's too much to ask of your skin, and you will undoubtedly nick yourself. Much better to do a proper wet shave in the morning, which will see you through until your date later in the day. See the tip box to get the most out of your shave.

SHAVING TIPS
- Wait until at least 15 minutes after you get up to have a shave – it makes a difference to the ease of shaving.
- Press a hot cloth on to your face for about 30 seconds to soften the beard.
- Use gel, foam or soap and let it soak in for two minutes to further soften your beard.
- Use a swivel-headed razor for the closest shave.
- Always shave in the direction of your beard growth and don't assume it is all one way.
- Work from the outside in, leaving the chin and neck to last, and go down as far as your Adam's apple.
- Splash your face with cold water, then pat dry.
- Don't apply aftershave immediately after shaving: it contains alcohol, which will irritate and dry the skin. Opt instead for soothing balms containing tea tree oil or menthol.

STUBBLE

If you want to go for stubble, invest in a pair of hair clippers or beard trimmers that give you a variety of options. Don't just think you can stop shaving for a few days and automatically look sexier: you will simply look unkempt. Stubble can look very sexy if you get it right, and it can give you more confidence if you have acne-scarred skin.

SIDEBURNS

These are quite a high fashion look, demand a lot of upkeep and require a huge amount of confidence to pull off. Don't ever make them too thin – they look stupid.

MOUSTACHE

There is a reason that not many men opt for moustaches any more: they look dated, more sad 1970s playboy than suave 21st-century man. Women generally hate the way it tickles when kissing, too.

GOATEE

This look, which includes moustache and chin beard, has to be trimmed daily, so it is too high-maintenance for lots of men. However, it is more contemporary than just a moustache.

CHIN-ONLY GOATEE

The most famous sporter of this look is Brad Pitt. It draws attention to the chin and lower face, and definitely looks better on a young guy. You need regular growth to avoid a straggly, hippy look.

FULL BEARD

While this is useful for hiding bad skin or bulking out a narrow face, it needs trimming every couple of days to keep the shape. Use hair conditioner on it to keep it soft.

Eyebrows

Eyebrows are the framing of your face, so do pay attention to them. They can enhance or ruin your look.

WOMEN – don't go out with unplucked brows: stragglers are never sexy. If you have never paid attention to your eyebrows before, get them shaped professionally, then just follow that line. Overplucked brows look old-fashioned and hard. If yours are sparse, pencil them in with a soft brown eye pencil and aim to create a soft arch.

MEN – don't think natural is OK. Get plucking if you have eyebrows that meet in the middle: women are suspicious of monobrows. Pluck just enough to create a finger-width gap at the top of your nose. To reduce the discomfort, numb the area by running an ice cube over it for a few minutes, then pluck in the direction of the hair growth. While you're at it, snip off any luxuriant nasal hairs with scissors – don't try and pluck them, it's way too painful – and also trim any sprouting ear hair.

Make up

It's easy to get confused by the huge amount of choice, scientific claims and seductive packaging of today's products, but your aim should be to keep it simple. It is not about the amount of money you spend (most of us have far too many products that we never use anyway). The key to looking good lies in using just a few products and applying them well.

BASE

This can be either a liquid foundation or a powder – there is no need to use both. It's old-fashioned to look as though you're wearing a mask. The modern approach favours 'barely there' bases that are used to even out skin tone. Get the colour right by trying it on your face (not your wrist or the back of your hand) and check it in daylight. It should merge seamlessly with your natural colour.

If you have oily skin, always look for products that are described as 'non-comodegenic', which means they won't clog up your pores. Apply water-based liquid foundations over mattifying lotion, or use oil-absorbing powders. If you have dry skin, go for liquid foundations with added moisture, or mix them with some of your own moisturizer before you apply it. If you want to camouflage signs of ageing, look for products containing light-reflecting pigments. These reduce the appearance of lines by making light bounce off the skin.

Don't apply foundation all over your face: put it just where it's needed to even out skin tone, and avoid the eye area, where products love to sit in creases. Several thin layers are more effective at covering problem areas than a single thick layer. Use sponges, fingers or brushes to apply.

CONCEALER

There is a huge selection of concealing products, so do try them out to get the best one for your skin. It's worth buying a palette of two or more concealers because you can mix the colours to match your skin tone at different times of the year. These products should hide spots, red veins and under-eye circles, and camouflage lines around the nose and mouth. (When hiding spots, apply concealer after your base.) Go easy round the eye area to avoid the concealer sitting in crêpy lines. Use a brush or finger in a rocking movement to build up a layer on your skin. Most women tend to use way too much, so be sparing and it should last for ages. If you want to hide birthmarks, blotches, age spots on hands, scars or pronounced thread veins on your face or body, use a medical concealer. It contains a stronger pigment and is a heavier product, so build up cover slowly.

BLUSHER

Colour applied to your cheeks helps to create a vibrant, youthful look. Aim to create a soft flush, like the glow you get when you've been outside in winter; forget all those heavy-handed contour tricks of the 1980s. Buy a pink powder blush (avoid orange or strong bronzes) and use a brush to sweep it over the apple of your cheeks. Cheek gel, sold in little tubes and applied with your fingers, is also good but it takes practice to apply correctly. Blondes should go for pale pinks and apricots, brunettes for rosy pink and redheads for bright pastels. Dark skin tones suit shades of plum; avoid pinks because they tend to look grey.

EYE SHADOW

Less is definitely more as far as eye make-up is concerned. For a simple modern look, cover your eyelid up to the brow bone with base or a neutral colour that matches your skin: this will open up your eyes and even out skin tone. Add a subtle eye shadow that makes your eyes shimmer; avoid bright colours, sparkle and glitter. Light, pearly shades are pretty and idiot-proof, so you can sweep them on with a brush or finger for sheer all-over colour. Avoid iridescent eye shadows because they accentuate wrinkles and saggy eyelids.

EYELINER

Add some definition by using a soft brown or grey (not black) eyeliner close to your upper lashes, and keep it looking soft. If you can't draw a straight line, cheat by drawing dots close together, then fill in the gaps with more dots. Try lining the eyes with a white pencil to make them appear wider.

MASCARA

Buy a mascara designed to lengthen rather than thicken, and apply to the top lashes only: this will prevent you from looking tired. Long Bambi lashes rather than spidery clumps are the look that's needed for Tracey's eye-batting tips. Lashes that are dark and curled make you look more wide-eyed, and are an essential if you're blonde.

To elongate lashes, build up mascara on the outer corners, which will also widen your eyes, and apply in an upward direction from lash line to tip. For more definition, wiggle the brush at the base of the lashes, then flick through the middle, not the ends. Black is a hard colour, so use it only if you are dark-haired. If you're blonde, go for dark brown. Whatever your colouring, never be tempted by the 1980s' Sloane look of navy blue.

LIP COLOUR

Our eyes are naturally drawn to plump soft lips, but don't despair if yours lack fullness; there are ways to cheat, and gloss is the key when it comes to perking up a flagging face. Avoid dark lipsticks in hard colours and matte textures because they accentuate thin lines. Go for lip glosses in caramel, toffee or subtle pink. Dark-skinned women can get away with brighter shades, but do avoid any that are super-shiny: men hate that gloopy look – it puts them off kissing.

No product outside a plastic surgeon's room can increase your lip size permanently, but etching round your lip line (never outside it) with a light-reflecting concealer pencil really makes a difference. Fill in your lips with a gloss lipstick or sheer colour wash: leave the solid colours behind when it comes to pouting success. If you already have a great mouth, go easy on your eyes and make your lips the focus of your face.

Teeth

Dirty stained teeth are never attractive, so if you haven't got the best smile ever, fix it. Oral hygiene is vital where there may be kissing involved, so you need to make some extra effort. A good white smile and healthy gums can also take years off your face, so there's no sensible reason for ignoring your mouth.

Lots of dental surgeries offer a huge range of treatments, and there are also plenty of products to use at home to help whiten your smile. Note that to see the effect, you'll need to start using them up to a week before your date.

Always clean your teeth before a date because plaque builds up during the day. Use dental floss or toothpicks to remove unsexy bits of food and bacteria that get caught between your teeth. It may be time-consuming, but it does mean you arrive feeling confident of fresh breath.

Nails

Men need to take care of their hands because women are definitely turned off by dirty nails and chewed cuticles. Use nail clippers to cut nails to a uniform length – easier to do after a bath or shower when the nails are softer. File the edges smooth so they don't catch on your clothes, and gently push back cuticles using the edge of a flannel or towel. Your hands will then look cared for rather than overly manicured, and you may even get a few compliments. If you are wearing open-toe shoes or sandals, please pay the same attention to your feet. Many a promising date has been ruined by the sight of a thick yellow toenail.

Women's nails have become a mini-industry, with manicure salons springing up all over the place. However, short and natural-looking are the key words here. Long nails look old-fashioned and cheap. Don't go on a date with dirty nails or chipped nail varnish. File nails to a uniform length and choose pale pink, beige or clear polish. Red looks tarty, and men just don't understand high-fashion colours, such as blue, green or purple. Save the bolder colours for your feet, especially if you're wearing open-toe shoes or sandals.

Body piercings and tattoos

The world is divided about the sexiness of these, so if you do have a tattoo or piercing that you are really proud of, be aware that not everyone will think it's great. In fact, it might be a good idea to let your date get used to it slowly. Wear discreet jewellery without sharp edges in piercings: this will help to keep the focus on you rather than your body statement, and ensure your date feels safe enough to get closer. Tattoos can be very useful flirting tools, as Jeremy points out on page 116, so promise a one-to-one viewing rather than revealing it all early on.

HOMEWORK:

FACE FACTS

Just as high street clothes shops are in a constant state of evolution, so too are make-up and product counters, which have undergone some changes in recent years. Nowadays, the people behind the counter are friendly and knowledgeable, so make the most of them. Everything they have on sale is for us to experiment with, so be bold.

- Visit a good department store or high street beauty products shop and browse through the different ranges.
- Ask for information and advice on the various products and try them out. You won't be pressurized to buy.
- Shop around until you find something that suits you.
- Don't be afraid to ask for samples before you purchase. It's a good idea to test products over a few days to make sure you are not allergic to them.

The big date

This is when the fun really starts. You know by now that there is no guaranteed blueprint for a 'result outfit'. Sexy dressing is about individual choice: it is not about wearing revealing clothes. *WLTM* guest Janine ended up in a trouser suit that revealed very little, but it made her feel the proverbial million dollars, which is what you should aim for too. Your date outfit should make you feel that you're oozing sex appeal. Remember, if you pay enough attention to your outfit, your date will pay attention to it too. Before you get dressed with confidence, ensure you make the right preparations, as outlined below.

Squeaky clean

Feeling fresh will enhance your confidence, so do leave time for a shower and hairwash.

HAIR

Don't ever be tempted to rub talcum powder into your greasy hair roots: shiny, newly washed hair always looks and smells better. Be careful when applying styling products, as it is easy to use too much.

Men – watch out for greasy hair pomades, waxes or laminators; they generally contain silicone and oil to make hair gleam and are good for giving texture and hold, but too much looks greasy and unattractive. No woman will want to run her hands through that.

Women – please do not use hairspray. It is old-fashioned and smells horrid, and however little you use your hair ends up with that rigid look universally hated by men. Your hair should be shiny and soft, making your date want to stroke it, not run away. If you have trouble keeping stray hairs in place, put a little spray on a cotton wool ball and rub over your parting and hairline.

This is not the day for forgetting to use a deodorant. Make sure you allow it time to dry before putting on your clothes or it could end up staining them. Do bear in mind that if you have just started using a crystal deodorant, they can take up to two weeks to be fully effective, so carry some back-up if you are still on the sweaty side. Take a small packet of deodorizing wipes, then you won't need to worry or try to sneak in any surreptitious under-arm sniffs.

As Tracey points out in Body Language, the mouth is always a focus of attention, so don't forget to brush your teeth before you go out. If you are worried about bad breath, rub your toothbrush over your tongue as well because bacteria can build up on the surface. Put some toothpicks in your pocket and when you go to the lavatory check for any stray bits of dinner still lurking between your teeth.

UNDERWEAR

Do make sure you wear the right underclothes beneath your date outfit.

Men – do you wear briefs or boxers? I've rooted through many a male underwear drawer and it is rare to find a man with a mix of both. I can never understand why, as different pants suit different trousers. If the trousers are fitted, don't bunch up boxers inside them – it looks suspicious. Also, don't show acres of pants above the waistband of your trousers – it won't impress anyone over 16. There is a whole world of choice in underwear, so take the time to update your collection. Check your back view in the mirror before you leave the house: it's not only girls who get visible panty lines, which is why they now make nude-coloured G-strings for men too. If you feel extra sexy by 'going commando', then do.

Women – If you are feeling self-conscious about carrying a few extra pounds, don't be tempted to wear control knickers that are in any way too tight: you will just bulge in other areas and look deformed. Big pants may well be comfortable, but do wear a pair of date knickers that make you feel sexy, even if you have no intention of your date seeing them later. To avoid visible panty lines, experiment with thongs. They can be a nightmare to begin with, so try buying a bigger size than you would normally wear. They give a really good look under tight trousers and skirts, and it's sexy to see just a hint of them at the back of low-cut jeans. Remember, your underwear should match your skin tone, not what you are wearing.

Make sure that you are wearing a bra that fits so there is no 'spillage'. If you are self-conscious about having big breasts, wear a minimizer bra and tighten the shoulder straps as far as you can bear for maximum uplift: it really works. If you need some extra padding, do make sure it can't be seen. Padded bras sometimes have seams that show under close-fitting tops, so go for gel-filled bras instead. Avoid the ones you pump up. WLTM guest Sam tried on a variety of enhancement bras and could not believe the difference it made when she chose the right one. However, she also remarked that some were unpleasant to wear: the pump-up ones went rock hard and looked false. Take the time and trouble to find the right one for you. If you are tempted by flesh-coloured jelly inserts, do remember that they tend to remain very cold against your skin. Make sure you insert them properly as they have a habit of escaping at very odd moments.

SCENT AND AFTERSHAVE

It is true that if you smell delicious, it provokes a positive reaction, but don't make the mistake of overwhelming your date with aftershave or scent. The idea is that they notice you smell great when they lean in towards you: they don't want to be engulfed in a miasma the second you come through the door.

Men – be aware that your chosen smell is available in different strengths. Aftershave is the weakest, cologne is the most concentrated, and eau de cologne falls somewhere between them, so apply accordingly. Also, do be aware that aftershave has the highest alcohol content, which can make it sting, so avoid using it on your face if you have dry skin. Put it behind your ears, on your chest or rub through your hair. Be aware of how many different aromas you can be wearing at one time and try to use matching deodorant, soap and aftershave.

Women – I can't stress enough that less really is more when it comes to smell. As a rule, stay away from overhyped power scents and find a fragrance that suits you. Nicole Kidman swears by her own mix of musk oil and vanilla, so take the time to find your signature scent. Be aware how many scented products you have on before adding your perfume: shampoo, conditioner, shower gel, body moisturizer and hand cream can all add up to a knock-out olfactory cocktail that can flatten your date at 20 paces.

Extra dating success

I know you might get to a stage of panic with so many things to remember all at one time on the date day, but it is worth taking five minutes out to make sure you have not forgotten anything and to run through a final check list of top date tips.

DO

- Pick an outfit that is suitable for the date venue.
- Be extra careful in a white top: it doesn't look good splattered with your starter or red wine.
- Avoid comedy clothes: T-shirts with jokey slogans, cartoon ties, novelty cufflinks.
- Wear trousers with a loose enough waistband: undoing your top button after the main course is not sexy.
- Wear some colour: it's the quickest way to get noticed (but women should avoid red on a first date because men take it as a sign of availability).
- Put tea tree oil or witch hazel lotion on spots to dry them up rather than squeezing them.
- Take a small amount of hand cream or moisturizer with you to control frizzy hair, but smooth it only through the ends.
- Wear sunglasses on your head if you're having a bad hair day.
- Make sure you compliment your date on their appearance.

You have absorbed a lot of style information since you started the homework, so make sure all your hard work pays off on your date. Don't make the mistake of falling into any old habits or any of the date style crimes listed below – which, of course, you would never do now!

DON'T

- Be tempted to overdress: understated is far better.
- Shop for a new outfit on the day of your date.
- Wear a suit unless you feel comfortable in it: looking uptight isn't sexy.
- Wear tights or socks with open-toe shoes or sandals.
- Wear too much jewellery: never more than two rings on one hand, and men – definitely no sovereign rings.
- Arrive carrying a bulging briefcase or massive sports bag.
- Have a radical new haircut on the day of the date.
- Take over-the-top presents.
- Reveal any personal body secrets.
- Wear sunglasses after sundown (except on a bad hair day, see above).
- Wear scuffed shoes: it negates all your other efforts.
- Be tempted to wear tight leather trousers.
- Wear top-to-toe linen: you will look a creased mess after 20 minutes.

This should give you all the ammunition you need for a wonderful evening, so now go and enjoy...

3

Confidence and communication

Jeremy Milnes

When you are next out, try this experiment. Close your eyes for 10 seconds and when you open them home in on the first person you see. Make sure your target is somebody you don't know. Now spend the next 30 seconds watching and listening. (For health and safety reasons it's a good idea to conduct this exercise discreetly: you don't want to risk giving offence.) OK, turn away and make a list of everything you can remember about that person. When you've finished, glance over it, and the chances are that it breaks down as follows:

50–70 per cent appearance
23–43 per cent tone of voice
7 per cent actual words spoken

Of course, these percentages hold true only for the initial meeting. After that the spoken word increases in value because talking is something we all love to do, isn't it? Well, it might have come naturally at school, and perhaps it still does with colleagues or friends. So when does it start to get difficult? Probably when you bump into that potential date at the health club, supermarket, dry cleaner's or wherever. What are you going to do? Spend the entire time looking each other up and down and smiling while you wait for your change or your clean shirt? No, you have to talk. But hang on a minute. You don't know this person. And besides, this is the UK: we're world famous for our reserve. We don't just start a conversation with anybody. Get on a train any day of the week and you'll see what I mean: carriages full of silence. Some people hide behind books or newspapers, others pretend to be asleep. You can almost see the signs over their heads: 'I don't talk to strangers.'

Sue, a contributor to *WLTM*, springs to mind here. I wanted her to practise initiating a conversation. The venue was a supermarket. Her task was to approach people as they were filling their shopping trolleys and strike up a conversation. After a few minutes it became clear that this was quite a challenge for Sue. I asked what was holding her back. 'People will think I'm mad. I wasn't brought up like this. You just don't go up and talk to people you don't know.' Train carriage syndrome strikes again.

At this point let me state loudly and clearly: if you are old enough to vote, drive a car, have sex (but not necessarily all at the same time), it's perfectly acceptable to talk to strangers.

Now, before you rush headlong into the dating arena, it's important to know what dating success is built on. In a word: confidence. It's essential to know where you stand on the confidence ladder, so do the quiz that follows and find out.

How confident are you?

How confident are you?

1. Whatever the job or task to be done, do you demand perfection from yourself?
   a. Always.
   b. Sometimes.
   c. Never.

2. If you're not successful at something, do you remain positive afterwards?
   a. Never.
   b. Sometimes.
   c. Always.

3. Are you the sort of person who can learn from your mistakes?
   a. Sometimes.
   b. Never.
   c. Always.

4. When you're with your friends, do you put yourself down in their company?
   a. Always.
   b. Never.
   c. Sometimes.

5. Are you a risk taker?
   a. Never.
   b. Sometimes.
   c. Always.

6. Do you generally expect to be successful in whatever you do?
   a. Sometimes.
   b. Never.
   c. Always.

7. A stranger pays you a compliment. Are you comfortable with this?
   a. Always.
   b. Never.
   c. Sometimes.

8. Are you one of life's conformers?
   a. Never.
   b. Sometimes.
   c. Always.

9. Something goes unexpectedly wrong for you. Do you blame other people?
   a. Sometimes.
   b. Never.
   c. Always.

10. Do you rely on other people's approval to feel good about yourself?
    a. Never.
    b. Always.
    c. Sometimes.

11. Do you compare yourself to other people and think, 'I wish I was them rather than me'?
    a. Always.
    b. Sometimes.
    c. Never.

12. As you walk along the street, somebody bumps into you. Do you apologize?
    a. Never.
    b. Sometimes.
    c. Always.

13. Does your inner voice tell you how wonderful you are?
    a. Sometimes.
    b. Never.
    c. Always.

14. Do you make plans to do something different from your usual routine, then later think up a dozen reasons why not to go ahead with it?
    a. Always.
    b. Sometimes.
    c. Never.

15. Do you generally expect things to turn out well?
    a. Always.
    b. Never.
    c. Sometimes.

16. Do you spend time smiling and laughing about life and taking it as it comes?
    a. Never.
    b. Always.
    c. Sometimes.

17. Do you believe that people want to listen to what you have to say?
    a. Never.
    b. Sometimes.
    c. Always.

18. A friend or flatmate suggests you throw an impromptu party. Would you do so?
    a. Always.
    b. Sometimes.
    c. Never.

19. A friend or colleague at work is in a bad mood. You don't know why but you can't help thinking it might be because of something you've done.
    a. Sometimes.
    b. Always.
    c. Never.

20. You know when you do something well and pat yourself on the back.
    a. Never.
    b. Always.
    c. Sometimes.

Add up your score.

1.   a. 3,   b. 2,   c. 1
2.   a. 1,   b. 2,   c. 3
3.   a. 2,   b. 1,   c. 3
4.   a. 1,   b. 3,   c. 2
5.   a. 1,   b. 3,   c. 2
6.   a. 2,   b. 1,   c. 3
7.   a. 2,   b. 1,   c. 3
8.   a. 2,   b. 3,   c. 1
9.   a. 2,   b. 3,   c. 1
10.   a. 3,   b. 1,   c. 2
11.   a. 1,   b. 2,   c. 3
12.   a. 1,   b. 3,   c. 2
13.   a. 2,   b. 1,   c. 3
14.   a. 1,   b. 2,   c. 3
15.   a. 3,   b. 1,   c. 2
16.   a. 1,   b. 3,   c. 2
17.   a. 1,   b. 2,   c. 3
18.   a. 3,   b. 2,   c. 1
19.   a. 2,   b. 1,   c. 3
20.   a. 1,   b. 3,   c. 2

If you scored 20–30...

Work is definitely needed but don't despair. You're not alone. Whatever has rocked your confidence, help is just a few pages away. Read the next section about confidence and get to grips with the homework tasks. They could change the way you see yourself, and how others see you.

If you scored 31–50...

Good going, but like every other living and breathing person, your self-confidence needs tweaking and tuning. I bet it can sometimes desert you, probably just when you need it most. It's time to get back on track and remember how good it can feel to be you.

If you scored 51–60...

Well done! Lack of confidence is certainly not holding you back. Check out the next section to avoid your wonderful self-confidence spilling over into unattractive arrogance. With your plentiful supply of self-belief, could it be your conversational skills that need work?

Confidence

So, after a long week at work, tonight is the night you've been waiting for.
You're ready to get out there and hit the bars, clubs, restaurants, wherever, in search of that gorgeous, mysterious stranger.

Dressed and ready to go, you catch a final glimpse of yourself in the mirror and your inner voice says, 'I look a million dollars. How can anybody resist me tonight?' You're ready to flirt, tempt and tease the night away. What can possibly stop you from meeting that special somebody tonight?

Well, to put it simply, you can. We've all been there. You spot the most attractive person standing at a bar or chatting away at a party and you wait for the right moment to make your move. And you continue to wait and wait until... Yes, you guessed it, somebody else acts on your indecision, moves in and another golden opportunity is lost. The following morning you stare in disbelief at yourself in the bathroom mirror, frustrated that you failed to seize the moment yet again. Why? You desperately wanted to get up and breeze in but that invisible wall of self-doubt, shyness, fear of rejection, call it what you will, kept you fixed securely in your safety zone. Once again you were unable and unwilling to take the risk. Does any of this ring true? You are not alone.

How do you recognize confidence?

Confident people usually display some of the following characteristics.
- A realistic outlook on life. They realize that everything can't always be perfect, and that's OK with them.
- A belief that they can't do everything; even when things go wrong they try to remain positive.
- An unwillingness to put themselves down – they know how damaging it can be and how unattractive it is.
- Take considered risks – after all, nothing ventured, nothing gained. Risk-takers are also attractive characters.
- Have a realistic expectation of success in their lives. They learn from their mistakes and move on.
- Feel comfortable when paid a compliment either by friends or total strangers.
- Don't feel restricted or constrained by the need to conform. Instead, they recognize and celebrate their own and others' individuality.

- Accept and are at ease with themselves, and take responsibility for their errors.
- Can live with disapproval. Their belief in their own abilities keeps them secure and grounded.
- Feel comfortable congratulating themselves without making a big show of it.

The point about confidence is that it comes and goes. You can be feeling great about yourself; life is fine, then suddenly wham! The roller-coaster plunges downward out of control and your confidence hits rock bottom. What makes this happen? Being dumped by your partner, losing your job, getting divorced, a bereavement, being told by 'friends' or even by your family that you're no good... Time can heal some battle scars, others fester.

Tony, an old friend of mine, was constantly compared unfavourably to his older brother when he was a child. Needless to say, he grew up thinking it was true, but he also felt inferior to everybody else he came into contact with. Not surprisingly, he had to put a lot of work into rebuilding his self-esteem and confidence, and unlearn a few false beliefs. His experience is a little extreme, but we are all susceptible to a loss of confidence and self-belief from time to time.

CONFIDENT OR ARROGANT?
It's important to recognize the difference between arrogance and confidence because those who lack confidence sometimes mix them up. Be careful. Arrogance is usually extremely unattractive.

Arrogant people tend to:
- Talk about themselves without really listening to others.
- Talk in a voice so loud that everybody can hear how wonderful and important they are.
- Draw attention to themselves.
- Need to be the centre of attention the whole time.
- Rarely talk about or take responsibility for mistakes they have made.

Arrogance is about being aggressive and overwhelming. Confidence is about being assured, trusting, self-reliant and bold. Which do you find the most attractive?

How to develop and boost self-confidence

Few people have climbed Mount Everest, won an Olympic gold medal or received the Nobel peace prize. In fact, the vast majority of us never do anything exceptional. We have to be realistic and accept that brilliance is a rare quality. Each of us achieves in our own way, and we must never undervalue our accomplishments. It's so easy to do though, isn't it? We begin to feel a bit low and before we know it, we start to focus on what we can't do rather than what we can do or have done.

As if beating ourselves up isn't bad enough, we then start comparing ourselves to other people, wishing we were as successful, intelligent or outgoing as they are. The bizarre thing is that the high-achievers have probably gone through the same process of self-doubt themselves.

Stop! Take your finger off the self-destruct button and make time for positive self-assessment:

- Stop reinforcing your negative beliefs (e.g. I'm a failure. I'll never find a partner).
- Stop telling yourself that you're not confident (e.g. I can't possibly join a salsa class to meet new people).
- Stop telling other people how hopeless you are. It gets tedious and sounds like you're after the sympathy vote.

Negative self-talk is destructive. Ignore the voice in your head that reinforces negative beliefs. You wouldn't let your friends talk to you the way you talk to yourself, so give yourself some praise – remind yourself of your achievements.

REVERSE THOSE THOUGHTS
Never underestimate the power of positive thinking. A little bit of self-encouragement can literally change your life. Acknowledge that you have the power by changing negative thoughts to positive ones.

I could	becomes	I can
I should	becomes	I will
I have nothing to say	becomes	I want to talk
I don't like meeting people	becomes	I want new friends
I can't do it	becomes	I'll risk it

Shyness and how to beat it

Research shows that up to 75 per cent of adults admit to feeling shy in one or more business or social situations, so it is not unusual. However, while a touch of reticence can be appealing, making you seem more interesting or mysterious, an inability to communicate is agony for you and a potential burden for others.

You don't have to live with shyness. You can do something about it.

Stop telling yourself that you are shy. This simply reinforces your negative belief.

Stop telling other people that you're shy. Will they find this an attractive quality? Probably not.

Stop talking yourself down. Negative talk is destructive.

Start talking yourself up. If you value yourself, others will too.

Start thinking positively. Ignore the voice in your head that reinforces negative beliefs about yourself.

SHYNESS-BUSTING TIPS

- Keep reminding yourself what you are good at – make a list.
- Help new people by teaching them your skills – you are the expert.
- Increase your social circle outside the family.
- Practise your voice variety skills at every opportunity (see pages 109–10).
- Smile and thank people who compliment you.
- Pay other people compliments.
- Spend time with people who make you feel good.

Assert yourself

Richard, our first gay contributor on *Would Like to Meet*, had a memorable dummy date for all the wrong reasons. For two hours he allowed himself to be verbally beaten up and belittled by his date, and for two hours he sat back and did absolutely nothing about it. Richard believed that, on a date, both parties should be polite and respectful to each other at all times. He is, of course, quite right, but sometimes it doesn't go according to plan. What Richard didn't appreciate was that it's OK to voice your own opinions, and it's equally OK to have a different point of view from your date. There were times when he took exception to what was said to him, and yet he remained passive. Finally, he could take no more, and became verbally aggressive. The dummy date limped to an awkward and uncomfortable end.

Richard needed to learn how to assert himself without losing control. Assertiveness sits comfortably between passivity and aggression; it's part of what makes confident people so at ease with themselves and around others. As a nation, we aren't that good at being assertive. Don't believe me? How many times have you wanted to complain about the food or service in a restaurant but sat back and said nothing?

In the best sense, and the one we should all aspire to, being assertive means being positive and forthright. In its negative sense it means being dogmatic and demanding. A degree of assertiveness is essential to all of us or we'll find ourselves overlooked and undervalued. This essential quality is built on four pillars:

Self-esteem: feeling good about yourself.

Self-knowledge: knowing how you feel about a situation.

Respect for others: listening carefully to other people's feelings and needs.

Communication: say clearly how you feel and what you would like to happen.

That's all very well, I can hear you saying, but how do I assert myself when I'm shy/nervous/out of practice? Well, if you've followed the advice on pages 103–8 and done the suggested homework, your confidence should be vastly improved. But you also need to approach the situation where you need to assert yourself thoughtfully and logically.

PREPARATION
- Think about the issue.
- Work out how you feel.
- Think about what you want.
- Prepare what you want to say.
- Practise saying what you want to say.
- Stay calm and confident.

ACTION
- Say what the issue is.
- Say how you feel about it.
- Say what you want to happen.
- Suggest specific actions.
- Listen to the response.
- Restate your case if necessary.
- Keep to the issue.

What Richard gained over his six weeks with the *WLTM* team was the ability to say what he thought and felt without being in the least bit rude. Gone was his fear that he would make himself unpopular if he dared to speak his mind.

HOMEWORK:

THINK POSITIVE

This exercise is designed to help you realize that your life is fuller than you think. Now don't start denying it before you've even started. Get a pen and a piece of paper and list 10 of your achievements. Take your time and think about all the things you have done or are doing that make you feel good about yourself. It doesn't matter how big or small they seem. Beside each achievement, write how it makes you feel about yourself. Your list might look something like this:

My achievements	My feeling
1. Passed my driving test	Successful
2. Helped neighbours to move	Useful
3. Learning to play guitar	Determined
4. Decorated the sitting room	Practical
5. Remembered my sister's birthday	Virtuous
6. Had dental check-up	Relieved
7. Praised by my boss	Competent
8. Was complimented on my haircut	Attractive
9. Complained about poor service in restaurant	Assertive
10. Went to a party	Brave

Now read through your list. How did it make you feel to remind yourself of your successes? It's important to recognize your accomplishments, no matter how minor. Spend some time every day on this exercise. Stick your list on the fridge or bathroom mirror, and keep a pocket version in your wallet or purse. Read it often and pat yourself on the back. And remember to update the list regularly. You'll discover that you're always achieving something and will gradually build up your self-esteem. Go on – congratulate yourself!

End result? He had an absolutely amazing final date. His conversation was charming and self-assured without being at all opinionated. And his date found him totally irresistible.

Time to take a risk

At the start of this section, I said that we have to be realistic in our expectations. For example, I'd love to be an astronaut but it's highly unlikely to happen now. I didn't even pass science at school. But wait a minute: should this stop me from even setting foot on the path of my dream or ambition? No.

Confident people take risks. I don't mean they hurl themselves out of planes or cross the Atlantic in a barrel, although some might. I mean they set new goals and challenges for themselves. Why? Because new experiences make life exciting.

'That's so interesting. I could never do that.' How many times have you heard people say something similar? Read between the lines and what they actually mean is: 'You're out there enjoying life. I find that attractive.'

It's important that you try to make your life stimulating because it will make you feel better about yourself. Also, new experiences mount up, like savings in a bank account, and they will give you more to talk about when you meet new people.

Go for it

Think of something you've always wanted to do, that would change your life in some way, but you've never got round to. It doesn't matter how grand it may seem. Whatever your dream, you can make it happen if you set yourself a series of steps to achieve it.

Let's take an example. Perhaps you have a secret ambition to go white-water rafting. Your first step might be going to the library or surfing the Net to find out more, such as does it require special equipment? Next, you could make a list of the places that have rafting holidays and start thinking about which country you'd like to visit. A bit later, you could visit the travel agent and get some brochures. It might also be worth seeing if the video shop has any films about it. Then you might find out if one of your friends would be interested in going rafting with you.

You don't have to do this all at once. Set yourself a realistic and achievable timescale for each step, but start tomorrow. Take a risk and set your adventurous spirit free.

Feeling ready for the world

This section has outlined some simple ways to build your confidence, but you have to work at them. Put yourself in situations where you practise what you've read and you'll be heading in the right direction.

Before you next go out to a party or find yourself in a PDS (potential date scenario), pause for a moment and check your confidence meter. Is it high enough? Are you running on full? Are you feeling self-assured, bold and ready to approach that special somebody? Are you feeling approachable? Can you walk up to that irresistible person and seize the opportunity?

If you can answer yes to these questions, you have created the foundations of a dating daredevil and can wave goodbye to the dating disaster.

HOMEWORK:

EYE-OPENER

For each letter of the alphabet, think of at least one word that describes your best or strongest qualities. This can be done with a group of friends who think of words for each other. (It's always fascinating to learn how others see you.)

This exercise is guaranteed to be a real eye-opener, as you will hear yourself saying, 'I never thought of myself like that before but now you say it...'

Voice

Have you noticed how some people can hold and engage you in conversation while others are in danger of sending you off to sleep? Which of these two categories do you think you fall into? This is a serious question, so think hard and be honest.

There's no need for anybody's voice to be a foolproof cure for insomnia, or for it to send people rushing to the nearest exit clutching their ears. Voices can be developed, and they should because – make no mistake about it – your voice is an in-built flirting tool.

Think of your favourite actor or singer. Now try to recall the sound of their voice in your head. Imagine them talking to you – telling you how much they've been looking forward to seeing you and how they've planned an exciting and mysterious evening for you both. Imagine not only what they say, but also the way they say it.

OK, you can stop now. Almost certainly you imagined their voice drawing you in and holding you. You couldn't help but listen. It might have sounded assertive, confident, powerful or just downright sexy. Whatever its quality, it seemed to flow through you and touch you, leaving a lasting impression. This is proof that the sound of a great voice is positively music to your ears.

Variety is the spice of life

This section is not about trying to turn you into an actor or a public speaker. It's concerned with helping you to make the most of your voice so that you sound interesting and confident. Some people seem to be able to vary the way they use their voice effortlessly and naturally. If that isn't the case with you, don't worry – help is at hand.

Simon, a contributor to *WLTM*, had some great topics of conversation on his dummy date. Travel was his thing, and his date shared the same interest. The conversation should have been crackling with electricity but his voice lacked the variety needed to enthuse his date by what he was saying. Instead of seducing her with his tales of faraway places, she was looking around, turning away and fidgeting, clearly wishing that she was somewhere far away. She was bored not by what he was saying but by the way he was saying it. There was no variety in his voice to spice up his conversation.

Warm up workout

Before launching into any voice work it is important to give your voice a gentle warm-up. I am grateful to Penny Dyer, a professional voice and dialect coach for this exercise. Penny has worked with a number of highly successful actors, including Cate Blanchett, Anthony Hopkins and Nicole Kidman. She recommends the following exercises to relax and prepare your voice.

- Lie on the floor and look straight up at the ceiling. This is important to ensure that your chin isn't tilted. Place your arms by your sides, palms facing upwards. Open your shoulders out. Close your eyes. Imagine you are on a beach listening to the ebb and flow of the waves. Breathe in silently through your mouth (never through your nose because you don't breathe in through your nose when you talk). Feel the coldness of the air on the back of your throat. As you breathe out, mirror the sound of the waves travelling up the beach by making a 'sssshhhh' sound.
- Now place one hand on your abdomen. As your breath 'drops' in, you should feel your hand rise; as you breathe out, your hand should fall. This is important because you must learn to breathe from your abdomen to make the most of your voice.

Do this exercise for five minutes or so, and listen to your favourite music if it helps you to relax. You can, of course, vary the sound you make when breathing out: try using 'mmmmm' or 'aaahhh' instead. This exercise will make you feel great, so do it regularly. It's worth it.

Introducing vocal variety

Variety can be achieved in different ways, so let's look at some of them.

Pace of delivery. Varying the speed and emphasis with which you speak makes the information you're imparting sound more interesting. A monotone will send your listener(s) into a coma no matter how fascinating the subject matter.

Volume. Speaking quietly can be a great technique to get people to move closer to you, but it's tiring for the listener if they have to strain to hear you all the time. Similarly, bellowing is stressful and potentially embarrassing if you're having a conversation in a public place.

Pauses. Stopping to think about what you're saying is necessary from time to time, but very long pauses will make your listener feel uncomfortable and bored. On the other hand, not pausing at all can make you sound mechanical and obsessive.

Changes in pitch. Using your vocal range will add emphasis and 'colour' to what you're saying. Without changing pitch, your voice will sound flat and uninteresting.

Record yourself telling a story, then listen to it carefully. If you think your voice is lacking any of these positive attributes, you must do something about it or you'll be missing out on a valuable dating tool.

Volume, pauses and pitch

Adding colour to your voice is important. If you don't vary the volume, pauses and pitch as you speak, you are in danger of flat-lining – speaking in a monotone – which will kill your conversation stone dead however exciting the subject matter. If you've ever had to listen to somebody drone on and on like a dripping tap, you will know exactly what I mean.

Used well, your voice can hold attention, surprise, excite and seduce your listener. It's like playing an instrument – with practise you can get the most from it.

HOMEWORK:

PUSHING THE PACE

In 1990 I trained for three months for the London marathon. My official training manual said that I should talk whenever I was running: if I could talk without getting breathless I was running at the correct pace.

If you're a slow and ponderous speaker, this same technique can be used to help you develop the pace of your conversation.

- Rope in a friend to go for a walk or run with you and ask them to vary the pace as you go along.
- Choose a topic that interests you and start telling your friend a story connected with it. (Simon, the contributor I tried this with, described his experience on a roller-coaster, which was a perfect choice for this exercise.)
- Ask your friend to react to what you're saying by making you walk or run faster as the story dictates. Almost without thinking, you'll find your voice injected with energy when the pace is increased for thrilling parts, and slowed down for quieter parts. Your story, which you might have told dozens of times before, will take on new life and interest when you vary the pace.

This is a great exercise because you can do it whenever you're walking, either out loud or in your head. Just make sure you have a clear road in front of you.

Have you ever noticed the way sports commentators use their voices? Their techniques break down as follows:

- They increase volume at moments of high tension or excitement.
- They decrease volume to draw the listener in and emphasize critical moments.
- They insert pauses for dramatic tension or to allow time for the listener to take in what has been said.
- They alter the pitch to convey enthusiasm.

You can try this for yourself by taping a favourite sporting event and listening carefully to the commentary to identify the variations in the commentator's voice. Replay the tape with the sound turned off and step into the commentator's hot seat. If you like, you can record your voice so you can examine your effort afterwards. This is a great way of practising your vocal skills.

Another way to work on your vocal range is to tell stories to that most critical and difficult audience – children. They'll soon tell you if you're flat-lining.

Singing is also a wonderful way to work on giving your voice more variety. It doesn't matter if you can't hit all the notes because you will simply be extending and using your voice, discovering what it is capable of. Sing along to a CD or belt something out on your own, but take care not to strain your vocal cords.

Vocal patterns cannot be changed overnight: it takes constant practice. If you are serious about making changes, you must practise every day. Don't be afraid to seek help from a qualified voice coach if you think you need it. An hour or so a week of professional coaching might be the best investment you'll ever make. Consult the Internet or the phone book to find your nearest practitioner.

VOCAL WORKOUT TIPS
- Warm up before you start work.
- Practise every day.
- Record your voice as you practise.
- Play your tapes to a friend or family member and ask them for an honest opinion. What differences can they hear?

Taking control

With your confidence high and your voice tuned, you now have the foundation stones in place to get out there and put them to the test. And that is exactly what you have to do – get out and meet people. Stop putting your social life on hold and wondering why you are on your own. The more people you come into contact with, the greater your chances of finding a date.

Getting out there

The world is unlikely to come knocking at your door, so you have to be pro-active, put your life into gear and move forward.

The obvious places to meet people are bars or clubs, but these may not be your idea of a fun night out. No problem. The dating scene has a huge range of venues: there's somewhere for everybody, so let's spend a few minutes considering where to go to find that special someone. Sit down and write out each of the headings below on a separate sheet of paper.

- Sporting events I go to or have always wanted to go to
- Sports I participate in or would like to take up
- Courses and classes I attend or have always wanted to enrol in
- Voluntary groups I am interested in joining
- Cultural events that interest me

Now do some serious brainstorming for 10 minutes. I think you'll be amazed at how many things you come up with. Everywhere you write down is a potential date venue. Once you have these lists, it's up to you to use them. Dating can't be done from the comfort of your armchair.

Don't limit yourself. Be daring, try new experiences and experiment with all that life has to offer. Don't assume you don't like something just because you've never tried it. Take Julie, for example. For years she said she hated football but had never attended a live match. Much against her better judgement, she went along to Stamford Bridge to watch Chelsea play. I'm not going to tell you that she is now a knowledgeable devotee of the beautiful game, but she did meet a guy at the match and she's been dating him regularly ever since.

And finally, consider this one. A couple of mates of mine go to beauty parlours once or twice a month for facials. They want to look their best, and why not? But they tell me it's also a great place to meet women.

Making a breakthrough

Somebody at some point has to take the initiative and start a conversation. You may be lucky and find people approaching you, but if you're not, what are the easy ways in? Perhaps you're thinking, 'There are no easy ways in. If there were, I wouldn't be reading this book.' Well, read on.

I remember working with a *WLTM* contributor called Jon. We were in north London and his task was to approach people and ask for directions to the London Eye. This was his ice-breaker or way in. Not too difficult a task, I thought, yet with cameras rolling, Jon delayed the moment, arguing that it was a false situation and that it made him feel uncomfortable. After much deliberation, he finally confessed that the real reason for his reluctance was fear of rejection.

This, of course, is a very real and understandable concern, and another good reason to ensure your confidence is up. Fear of rejection can lead to a state of high anxiety if you let it. Avoid that by telling yourself, 'Yes, I might be rejected but so what? It really isn't the end of the world.'

And don't forget that there could be a whole host of reasons why somebody doesn't wish to talk. Perhaps they want time to themselves, they're in a hurry or have had a bad day at work. Don't take it personally and don't let it get to you. It really isn't worth it. I promise you there will be plenty of women and men who will be delighted to chat with you. Once Jon had broken through his reluctance, he was amazed at how easy it was to talk to people. You will be too.

Starting a conversation

Approaching a stranger and striking up a conversation might seem daunting, especially if you're out of practise. Keep things light and you'll find that most people respond well to friendly overtures. To make things even easier, try using some of the opening gambits outlined below.

OPENER 1: ## The Californian approach

Last summer I travelled alone around California for six weeks. Americans, I discovered, can and do talk to anybody. A typical conversation starts with 'Hi, how you doing?'

I showed *WLTM* contributor Simon this approach when we were in a bar. We spotted six women chatting and laughing, clearly in party mood. I walked over to their group, made eye contact and smiled. When a smile was returned I knew it was safe to move to stage two.

'Hi. What's the celebration?'

'It's my sister's birthday. We're having a night on the town.'

Success! Initial contact made. Simon and I spent the next hour joining in the birthday fun.

When you use the Californian approach:

- Walk over to the person you want to talk to.
- Smile.
- If they smile back, seize the moment.
- Say hello.
- Introduce yourself.
- Ask an easy-to-answer question (see pages 123–4).

This approach takes courage but bear this in mind: whoever you talk to will think you are incredibly brave to make this move. It's a bit like walking a tightrope without a safety net, but it's also fun. Go out with a friend and try it.

OPENER 2: Mood matching

Before you start a conversation with somebody, take a few moments to assess his or her mood. If they seem full of energy, the chances are their conversation will be too, so match it. If they appear quiet and reserved, a turbo-charged conversation might not be appropriate, so approach things in more subdued mode. Mood matching is the conversational equivalent to Tracey's body mirroring (see page 45).

OPENER 3: Expert advice

Asking for help, guidance or clarification is a sure-fire winner in opening a conversation. It doesn't mean you're dumbing yourself down – you're simply allowing somebody to take on the role of expert. Most people love this because it makes them feel important and special. Here's an example of how it works.

On one *WLTM* programme I went with our contributor, Debbie, to Wimbledon Dogtrack. She enjoyed a flutter, but knew very little about the dogs, so her task was to ask people to explain the race card to her. Her opener was honest and genuine, so she felt comfortable using it. She was also among enthusiasts, so establishing a common interest was not a problem. Without exception, every person she asked was delighted to help.

Debbie was amazed at how easy it was to start chatting with people using this opener. She was equally surprised at the positive responses she got. Wimbledon Dogtrack is now one of her favourite places on the dating circuit.

Wherever you are, be it out shopping, in your local gym, wandering round a museum or sitting in a coffee bar, try asking an 'expert' for advice. I doubt you'll be disappointed.

OPENER 4: **Eyes wide open**

This means just what it says. Keep your eyes open to find conversation openers. Imagine you're having a quiet drink when your attention is drawn to that interesting person standing at the bar. You take in the full picture and notice that a computer magazine is tucked under the person's arm. There's your opener, right before your eyes. You can either cast them as the expert – 'Excuse me, is that magazine any good? I need to find out about computers.' – or match their mood by sharing their interest – 'I see you're into computers. Me too.' You might even say, with a smile on your face, that computers are beyond you and then ask what people find so fascinating about them.

How you start is completely up to you, but the eyes-open approach is great because the recipient is flattered. It says 'I've noticed you.'

You can adapt this opener to fit any object: camera, mobile phone, personal music system or recent shopping purchase. This approach works well because the opener is realistic and safe.

Don't panic if the person on the table next to you isn't carrying an opener object. There's another way in, but it does require a little more courage: 'I really like your shirt/top/watch/ring/coat. Where did you get it from?' Again, you're paying an indirect compliment, which is easy to give and will make the person feel special.

I suggested this approach to *WLTM* contributor Simon when we were in a bar. The girl he wanted to talk to had a small tattoo on her shoulder, so he approached her and said: 'That's a great tattoo. I've never seen one like that. Where did you get it done?' The ice was broken…

OPENER 5: **The hand of fate**

This gambit may keep you waiting around for an awfully long time. On the other hand, it can occur at the least expected moment. If it does, take full advantage of it. Seize the moment!

Let me tell you what I mean. A year or so ago I went to see a band at Wembley arena. I was standing at the bar with a few friends before the show when two women caught my eye. They were chatting away to each other, clearly looking forward to the night ahead. I wanted to get to know them but felt uneasy at the thought of just going up and saying 'Hi.' We were at the same concert, so we had something in common to chat about, but it was the ice-breaker I needed. I noticed that they were flicking through the concert programme, so I could have used that as my 'in': 'Excuse me, where did you get your programme, please?'

Then fate stepped in. One of the women (the one who had really caught my eye) dropped what looked like a cheque from her handbag as she searched for her cigarettes. She hadn't noticed. Here was fate handing me my opener on a plate. All I had to do was walk over, pick up the cheque and say, 'Excuse me, you dropped this.' Striding forward confidently, a full glass of beer in hand, I made my move. I bent down to pick up the cheque, a smile of success already breaking out on my face. As I did so, I lost my footing and stumbled, spilling the entire contents of my glass over both women. Not the best start. Expletives rained down on me thick and fast. Sheepishly, I returned the cheque, apologized profusely and beat a hasty retreat back to my friends who had witnessed the entire episode with great amusement.

After the concert we were sitting outside a local bar going over the events of the night when who should drive past in a line of traffic but the two same women. Fate had stepped in again. The traffic lights changed to red and their car stopped. Putting down my drink, I ran across to their stationary car and invited them to join us. They accepted, and from that moment Sue became and remains a very special friend.

All these openers are generic. They can be used to meet people at work or when you're out socially (but see the extra information about parties on pages 118–20).

HOMEWORK:

SMART WAYS TO GET DATES

Ask anyone the best way to meet new people and they'll almost certainly suggest joining a new group, club or society. Set yourself SMART targets to do this.

Specific –	I will join a health club.
Measurable –	I'll go twice a week, on Mondays and Thursdays.
Appropriate –	Yes. I'll meet new people and get fit at the same time, something I've wanted to do for ages.
Realistic –	Definitely. A great new club has just opened down the road.
Time –	I'll join within the next two weeks.

Although it may be very tempting to pick up the phone and plan to do this with a friend, resist that temptation. Go alone so you have to meet new people. It's an ideal opportunity to practise some of the opening gambits discussed earlier.

Party parlance

The easiest place to initiate a conversation with somebody has to be at a party. We go to parties because we want to meet new people. If we didn't, we wouldn't be there in the first place. So everybody at the party should be open to talking. However, there are ways in which you can help yourself.

CIRCULATE
Move around the party alone or with a friend. See who's there and let yourself be seen. Smile and make eye contact with people.

BE APPROACHABLE
Don't stand round in a closed circle with a bunch of friends. It closes you off from others. You might as well put up a 'Keep Out' sign.

WORK THE PARTY
Wall-hugging sends out the wrong signals and won't get you very far. Even at a party you might need to be pro-active.

RESEARCH YOUR TARGET
After thoroughly circulating and taking in the talent, how do you break the ice? The easiest way is to ask your host for a few details about your intended target – where they live, what they do, what their interests are, how your host knows them, anything that can be used as an 'in.' Please be diplomatic, though. Don't search for personal information or you'll sound like some kind of stalker.

MAKING YOUR RESEARCH WORK
Remember, people expect to talk at a party, so walk up to your target and start talking. It might go something like this:

> 'Hi. I'm Sean.'
> [Wait to see if the person tells you their name. If they do, use it.]
> 'I'm Angela.'
> 'Nice to meet you, Angela. Mark [the host] tells me you're into music. He says you're a really good singer.'

This approach works because what you're actually saying is 'I've made the effort to find out something about you because I find you attractive.' This in itself is flattering, but then you follow it up immediately with a compliment – and who doesn't like to receive a compliment?

All you need to do now is wait for the response and you're away.

FLATTER, FLATTER, FLATTER

I cannot emphasize how important flattery is as a way of initiating conversations at parties. People usually make some kind of effort to look good when they go out, and they love people to notice. This holds true for men and women. Look at this example.

'Hi, I'm Sarah.'

'I'm Pravin.'

[Use their name in your follow-up]

'I couldn't help but notice your jacket, Pravin. I really like it. I've never seen one like that before. It looks great. Hope you don't mind me mentioning it.'

Mind? They'll positively love it! They'll probably spend the next few minutes giving you more information. Why? Because you have effectively said 'There is something distinctive about you/You stand out in a crowd/I noticed you.'

THE COMMON LINK

If you want a less risky approach, use a common link to start the conversation, namely the people throwing the party.

'Hi. I'm Maggie'

'I'm Charlie.'

[Use their name in your follow-up]

'I don't think we've met before have we, Charlie? How do you know Kate and David [the hosts]?'

Parties are meant to be fun, so don't treat chatting as though it's hard work. Listen to what you hear and respond naturally. It may not lead to love, but you'll make lots of new friends.

PARTY LINES

When you're at a party, use whichever conversation opener suits you best or seems right at the time. If you want to make a good impression, remember the following:

Don't
- Sound as if you are complaining or moaning.
- Sound rude or aggressive.
- Use cheesy chat-up lines.

Do
- Smile.
- Have a sense of humour.
- Sound bright and positive.
- Sound genuine.
- Have a great time!

Humour

Talking positively yet realistically about yourself and keeping conversation both light and upbeat is sexy. Some people have an added bonus – the ability to make people laugh, which can be super-sexy. Most of us enjoy being in the company of someone who can make us laugh, but funny people must be careful not to over-egg the pudding.

Paul, on *WLTM*, relied almost entirely on his sense of humour in social situations. He referred to himself as 'Comedy Paul' and people loved his company. Unfortunately, women rarely saw him as serious date material. Instead, he was always seen as a 'good mate, a good-for-a-laugh guy'. It was a case of 'Will the real Paul please stand up,' because it was virtually impossible to get behind the machine-gun fire of his jokes. This became apparent when I filmed a conversation task with him at a car boot sale. I had a lot of fun and he certainly made me laugh, but I didn't feel that I knew anything about him after being in his company for a whole day, other than that he was a natural comedian. His incessant 'funnies' also exhausted me. I felt like saying, 'Stop! Enough! Cut the act!'

Questions nagged away at the back of my mind. Why couldn't he ever drop the façade? What was 'Comedy Paul' hiding? The answer was simple. He felt that people would find the real Paul dull, so he hid behind his wit.

If you can make people laugh, you have a great gift, but just remember that people will also want to get to know the real you.

Small talk

It's a glorious summer afternoon and a friend has invited you to a barbecue. 'You have to come. There'll be lots of new people for you to meet.'

Armed with your bottle of Chardonnay, you arrive and can already make out the sound of people talking and laughing as you ring the bell. A complete stranger opens the front door. (Why is it that hosts rarely open the door at their own parties?) Making your way into the back garden where it's all happening, you're welcomed by your host and spend the next 15 minutes chatting and getting the lowdown on the other guests. Three chicken drumsticks and a couple of drinks later you're ready for action. You begin circulating, smiling as you catch people's eye. The most attractive person in the garden approaches you and you can't believe your luck.

'I hope you won't think me rude but I've been told that you…'

You've been researched! Flattered or what? You exchange a few words, but then disaster strikes. You can't think what to say next. How on earth do you develop the conversation? You don't feel confident in your ability to let things gradually unfold and just go with the flow. Several uncomfortable pauses later, you make your excuses and head for the safety of the bathroom. Another one bites the dust.

One of our contributors to *WLTM* had just this conversational block. Shungu, an intelligent and articulate law student, said that she had no idea how to make small talk. Her friends said if she managed to get past 'Pleased to meet you' with a guy, she would launch straight into a debate about recent changes in European law. It was hardly surprising that she left all potential boyfriends scurrying for the door. Her conversation was just too intimidating.

Now don't misunderstand me. I'm not saying that thought-provoking and challenging conversation is a bad thing – far from it. Most of us enjoy stimulating conversation, but at the right time.

Sue, another contributor, thought that chit-chat was trivial and a waste of time. She felt it had no purpose. As a result, if she did speak to people she hadn't met before, she came across as blunt and harsh. Even her own friends said that when they first met her they felt intimidated. Sue was simply frightening potential dates away.

Don't underestimate how important small talk is in the dating game. Small talk should be light, easy and certainly non-threatening. The sort of things we talk about might range from the latest films, books and plays to travel, restaurants and music. In fact, you can talk about virtually anything as long as the topic is up-beat.

If this seems trivial to you, ask yourself how we get to know people. The answer is through small talk. Please don't dismiss or underestimate the potential pulling power of everyday chit-chat. It's a way of making a positive impression, so it's very important that you know how it works.

Small talk techniques

Finding out about somebody involves asking questions. We all like people taking a genuine interest in us, so don't be afraid to ask. Also, if you do feel a bit self-conscious, asking questions takes you out of the spotlight for a while.

TECHNIQUE 1: CLOSED QUESTIONS

The simplest way to chat is to use closed questions, which require only yes or no answers. They don't dig very deep, so don't overuse them or the conversation won't move out of first gear. However, the response depends on who you're talking to. I have found that some people reply to a closed question with a yes or no, but then happily go on: 'Yes, because...' or 'No, and let me tell you why...'

But what if you aren't lucky enough to be talking to someone like this? You might find yourself in a closed-question conversation that goes along these lines:

A: Do you live round here?
B: Yes. Do you?
A: Yes. Do you like it?
B: No. Do you?
A: Yes.
[Silence]

Hardly stimulating stuff, I think you'll agree, so it's time to try an alternative conversational gambit.

TECHNIQUE 2: OPEN QUESTIONS

Using open questions is great because they require more than a one-word answer. They develop the conversation and move it forward. Open questions usually begin with the words how, why or what.

Let's go back to our 'Do you live round here' conversation and throw in a couple of open questions.

A: Do you live round here?

B: Yes? Do you?

A: Yes. How long have you lived here?

B: Nearly three years now.

A: What made you move here?

Bingo! We're moving up the conversational gears.

TECHNIQUE 3: 'WHAT IF' QUESTIONS

These are personal favourites of mine because they really do give you an insight into the person you're talking to. They are also fun and can turn the conversation into a bit of a game.

A: I moved here because I was fed up living in London. I really like it here. What about you?

B: I moved here because of my job. What if you could live anywhere? Where would you live?

A: Brazil. In a little house by the beach. What about you?

B: That's a tough one. Probably in a lighthouse in Scotland. Why would you choose Brazil?

A: Because…

See how this kind of question really opens up the small talk?

TECHNIQUE 4: CLICHÉD QUESTIONS

Now I deliberately used the 'Do you live round here?' question as an example because this would be a perfectly easy and natural question to ask somebody you've just met. Yes, I know it's a bit clichéd, along with asking what somebody does for a living or what they do in their spare time, but these are expected questions and therefore not intimidating. My advice would be to start with clichéd questions but develop them with open questions and 'what if' questions to move the conversation beyond the superficial.

When I was working with *WLTM* contributor Louise, I asked her, 'What would be the first five questions you would expect somebody to ask you if they were interested in you?' Without hesitation she replied, 'My name, where I live, what

I do, what I do in my spare time and whether we can meet again.' She wasn't wrong.

I always ask for a name quite quickly into a conversation and give mine in return because I think it's polite. I would also use the person's name from time to time as we chat because it helps to build the relationship. It adds a personal touch that makes people feel special and memorable. How flattering is that? But take care. Over-using someone's name is irritating and ultimately worthless. Don't devalue the currency.

There is one clichéd question that you need to handle with care: 'What do you do for a living?' Some people prefer not to talk about their work, so if you sense a reluctance to share this information, change the subject. If, however, you get the green light, use open questions to bring a sense of fun and exploration into your small talk.

A: What do you do for a living?
B: I'm a teacher.
A: Really?
B: And you?
A: I'm a nurse.

OK, so it's a fairly average exchange, and one that most of us have probably experienced at some time or another. However, by applying our open and probing questions, we can find out a great deal more about each other. Here's how:

A: What do you do for a living?
B: I'm a teacher.
A: What do you teach?
B: Drama.
A: That's a great subject. What made you become a drama teacher?

With just that one question you are not only showing a genuine interest but also pushing the clichéd question beyond the superficial and delving a little deeper. Notice as well the indirect use of flattery: 'That's a great subject.' The message you're sending is 'I find your job attractive.'

After the clichés are done and dusted, small talk usually follows a pattern of exchanging facts about ourselves, opinions about the topics that crop up in conversation and, finally, feelings. I cannot emphasize too much how important it is to bring your feelings into your small talk. Yes, it can be risky, and yes, you have to be selective about what you disclose. But a conversation devoid of emotions reveals nothing of who you are – your hopes, dreams, aspirations, what makes you excited, what makes you laugh, what makes you unique.

Let me use one of our contributors as an example. Jon was a trained journalist, used to getting information from people but very guarded about sharing his feelings. His conversation never seemed to progress beyond imparting facts and opinions. He couldn't see the point of bringing his feelings into small talk. Finally, we made the breakthrough. In a brief conversation with a woman at a bus stop Jon shared with her how beautiful and exciting he found the London Eye and the Eiffel Tower: they really stirred his emotions. The woman told Jon that she felt the same. Brief encounter over, I asked Jon what he felt he'd discovered. He thought for a second before replying with a grin on his face, 'I felt that sharing our feelings brought us closer together.' Thank you, Jon. Good point very well made. It's worth remembering.

SMALL TALK KEY POINTS
1. Take the risk – what does it matter if you're rejected by a stranger? There could be many reasons why.
2. Be active rather than passive. Initiate conversations. Be the first to say 'Hi'.
3. Look for receptive people who display open body language, use eye contact and smile.
4. Ask easy-to-answer questions. Ritual questions break the ice and are non-threatening.
5. Notice something positive about the stranger – what they are wearing, doing or saying – as a way in.
6. Use something they are carrying as a conversation opener.
7. Keep a list of closed and open questions in your pocket.
8. Introduce yourself and ask for the person's name. Use their name in your response.
9. If your clichéd question gets a brief response, use another to get a more enthusiastic response.
10. Remember that small talk establishes friendships and relationships. Small talk can lead to big talk.

Active listening

A successful conversation requires a balance between speaking and listening. Being bombarded with information is overwhelming and a little insulting. It suggests that the speaker is self-absorbed and has no interest in finding out about you. On the other hand, not talking enough is lazy and also slightly insulting. It suggests the speaker can't be bothered to make an effort to get to know you better.

When you listen to somebody talking you need to show that you are involved and interested in what is being said. Active listening is a skill that requires you to have your senses finely tuned. Don't think you can switch off for a moment just because it's not you doing the talking. When actively listening, you need to signal to the speaker that you're doing so, and this can be done in several ways.

SIGNAL 1: PROMPT

Give the occasional nod to show that you're listening. Also, use para-verbals, such as 'Aha' and 'Mmm'. Combined, these prompts send a very clear message that says, 'I'm listening, I'm interested, carry on.'

SIGNAL 2: EYE CONTACT

This is one that I know Tracey will back me up on. When you are listening attentively, look into the eyes of the person speaking. Let your eyes say 'I'm fascinated/interested/touched by what you say.'

SIGNAL 3: PAUSE FOR THOUGHT

A very slight pause for thought shows that you've been listening closely and want to consider before you speak. Don't get anxious if an occasional silence punctuates your conversation. Consider it as time out for thought and reflection.

SIGNAL 4: ACTIVE RESPONSE

Use remarks such as 'Really', 'That's fascinating', 'Amazing', 'I'm impressed' and 'Incredible'. Your aim is not to interrupt or take over the conversation. You are just prompting and flattering at the same time.

SIGNAL 5: ECHO

People with counselling skills call this paraphrasing. What you do is take the essence of what has been said, perhaps the parts that interested you the most, and slightly paraphrase what you heard. For example:

A: So, I joined a scuba-diving club a couple of years ago. I'd always wanted to learn to dive but had never been able to find the time. I'm really pleased that I took it up. It's brilliant. My first dive in clear seas when I was in Egypt was unforgettable.

B: You learnt only recently and yet you've already dived in Egypt! Sounds amazing.

Active listening also involves listening for areas of common interest to talk about and share. Take the example above. The response could have been:

B: You've dived in Egypt! Sounds amazing. I've always wanted to learn scuba-diving. How did you get started?

Notice that while a common interest is shared, an open question helps the small talk to move on.

SIGNAL 6:   ICEBERG STATEMENTS

I don't know who came up with this phrase but I love it because it describes so accurately what you should be actively listening for.

Have you ever been in a conversation when somebody has said something like 'I had such a weird night last night' or 'My weekend was really special'? You're left wanting to know what was so weird or special, but that's all you get. That is an iceberg statement. You are teased with the tip, but you are invited to go under the surface to find out what lies beneath.

With these newly acquired skills, you will never again feel the need to fill every silence with non-stop self-talk.

Self-disclosure

Having got the balance right between speaking and listening, what do you actually tell somebody about yourself when you first meet? I suggest you keep it fairly light. Don't talk about your traumatic childhood or colourful track record with the opposite sex. Similarly, don't exaggerate the truth because you will be caught out eventually. It's OK to disclose a few not-too-serious faults, but present some positive qualities too. After all, you're trying to present a balanced picture of yourself, not project an image of perfection. You don't want to scare

HOMEWORK:

CONVERSATION SKILLS

Having established that conversation involves both talking and listening, there are several things you can do to improve your skills.

- Listen to a good chat show host, such as Michael Parkinson. His skill is that he asks thoughtful questions, listens actively and picks up on iceberg statements.
- Try writing a dialogue between two people meeting for the first time. Write in closed and open questions, and include prompts and stage directions that focus on other active listening skills. Then read the dialogue through with a friend and discuss how well it works. When you feel that you've got a grasp of the techniques, get out there and put your new skills into practice.

people away or not be taken seriously. Keep it real and make sure that whatever little secrets you choose to reveal about yourself don't fall into the wrong hands. The aim is to engender mutual trust and respect.

Asking the big question

You are now just five words away from your date. All you have to ask is 'Can I see you again?' And yet for many people, asking that question remains the ultimate challenge. The secret is to downsize it in your mind. Don't think of it as such a big deal. Just remind yourself that you have already done all the hard work. Your confidence, voice, conversation openers and small talk skills have taken you this far, so how tough can the next bit really be?

Here's an example of how you might go about asking to see somebody again. I was on a train coming back to London one wet Sunday afternoon. It was packed with football supporters returning from a big game in Cardiff. I was standing with a group of people and we started a conversation to pass the time. I can't remember what we were talking about, football probably. What I do remember is that the woman standing next to me caught my eye. She had a warm smile, friendly face and was chatting away confidently. We introduced ourselves to each other and shared small talk until our train arrived in London. We walked down the platform together, each step bringing us closer to going our separate ways. I felt that we had got on well and I sensed that she felt the same. She was fun to be with and I enjoyed her company. I wanted to see her again. How could I ask her? I guess it was a matter of being totally honest. The big question conversation went like this:

Jeremy: It was really fun talking with you. I'm glad we met.
[Honest compliment.]
Wendy: Thank you. I'm glad too.
[Signs are good. Move to phase two.]
Jeremy: Perhaps we can meet up for a coffee? Can I give you my number?
[No pressure. She can take it and rip it up later if she wants.]
Wendy: Sure.
[Good! Write down number carefully so that it's legible. Remember to write my name next to it in case she forgets who I am.]
Jeremy: Look forward to seeing you again. Nice meeting you. Bye.
Wendy: Bye now.
[Smile, turn and go. Try not to look too excited.]

And that was that. Note a couple of key points in that big question manoeuvre.

- I gave Wendy a genuine compliment.
- I suggested meeting again but without putting her under pressure.
- I offered my phone number, I didn't ask for hers. This gave her the option of calling me if she wanted to. Women, for obvious reasons, might not like to give out their phone numbers to men they hardly know, so guys, always offer yours first.
- I finished with a compliment.

What happened next? Three or four days later Wendy sent me a text message. It read, 'Hi. It's Wendy. Here's my number. Call me if you'd like to meet up.' I looked at the message and a couple of things struck me.

- Text messaging allows you to remain distant. It's a great device if asking to see somebody again over the phone makes you nervous. Also it's personal without being over the top.
- She sent me her number and worded her message in such a way that I was offered the option to call her. Good move. I could, after all, have had second thoughts about seeing her again.

And that's how easy asking to see somebody can be.

The one question that I've left unanswered is 'What happens if I ask the big question and get turned down?' Simple. You pat yourself on the back for meeting somebody new and practising your conversation skills, and say in a loud, confident voice 'So what?'

No matter who you are, you're likely to be nervous about meeting your date. But nerves are OK – in fact, they can work in your favour rather than against you.

Actors get worried if they don't feel nervous before a show because an adrenaline rush can bring out their best performance. The same applies to you. Spend time preparing yourself, visualizing the date and thinking it through. For example, how will you greet your date? A handshake is safe, but be prepared to accept a kiss on the cheek. What will you start talking about? Asking what sort of day your date has had is a good safe question. Or perhaps you could talk about the restaurant. Will you have an aperitif or wait to have some wine with the meal? What sort of food will you order? Remember that the menu can give you conversation ideas: is your date a vegetarian, do they like pasta, have they ever been to Italy?

We do this sort of forward thinking all the time in other situations, imagining what might happen and how we'll deal with it. Think in advance about some topics you might want to discuss. This will help you to come across as confident and natural. Compliment your date on some aspect of their appearance, or ask them about something that they mentioned when you first met or spoke on the phone – a great film they'd seen, for example. Remembering details will make them feel special and is guaranteed to impress. If you think it will help, come up with a few pre-planned questions, but be careful as trying to remember them might add to your nerves.

ASKING SOMEONE OUT
Remember the following, and you'll be far less likely to meet with a refusal.

DO
- Pay a compliment before asking.
- Downsize the task. Imagine you're talking to a friend.
- Men, offer your number rather than expect a woman to give you hers.
- Suggest an easy first date, such as meeting for coffee or a drink.
- Sound enthusiastic but don't go over the top.
- End with a compliment.
- Have a pen at hand.

DON'T
- Sound as if you couldn't care less.
- Put pressure on yourself.
- Expect a woman to give her number first.
- Give the impression that you have a long-term relationship in mind, even it's what you're secretly hoping for.
- Throw out your arms and attempt a snog.

Hot dates and good manners

At the end of every show Jay, Tracey and I get very excited when we meet our contributor before the big date. It's a proud moment for all of us because we see such a transformation. If we've done our jobs properly, the final date should be a stunning success. Our parting words to each contributor are reminders and straightforward advice – and that's what I want to leave you with too in the last part of this book.

TOPICS TO AVOID ON A DATE

If you're in any danger of suffering from verbal outpourings on your date, make sure you steer clear of conversation clangers – they have dating disaster written all over them. What are they? Here's my top five.

CLANGER 1: ILLNESS

'I just sat on the loo all night. I couldn't move. It was awful.'
This is hardly a winner over dinner. Best avoid all talk of personal disasters on a first date.

CLANGER 2: DEATH AND BEREAVEMENT

'I'd had him since I was five. It was so sad when I eventually had to have him put down. I want to cry every time I think about him. Have you ever owned a gerbil?'
Sad your loss may have been, but do you need to share it now? Death, whether of animals or people, is an unhappy subject, so don't go there.

CLANGER 3: POLITICS

'So I spent the whole of the summer door-to-door canvassing for my local MP. You wouldn't believe the number of doors I've had slammed in my face. Oh, I knew I recognized you from somewhere…'
Political affiliations are sensitive subjects. You need to know someone very well before you tread on this delicate ground.

CLANGER 4: RELIGION

I think all the reasons for avoiding this subject are too obvious to outline here, and anyway, I'd hate to offend. I'm with Dave Allen on this one: 'May your God go with you.'

CLANGER 5: YOUR EX

'It was a brilliant relationship. We had so much in common. We loved each other desperately. And the sex…unbelievable! Now, what were you going to say about Viagra?'

Don't make your date feel inadequate by venturing into this territory. On the other hand, if you spend the whole evening running down your ex, your date will be wondering when it's their turn to be in the verbal firing line. Just don't go there.

All these conversations can be put on hold for a later occasion. First date conversation should be light, fun and flirty. If you do find yourself entering the realm of heavy topics, try to move the conversation back to lighter subjects. You'll have a better chance of seeing your date again if you avoid these touchy topics.

Date downers

Now you have the conversational side of the date sorted, don't get complacent. There are lots of other ways to sabotage the date without meaning to. Here are some things you should avoid doing if you want to make a good impression.

EXPOSING TOO MUCH

I'm not talking about cleavage or biceps here. I'm talking about giving too much information about yourself too soon.

If you went to the cinema and the entire plot of the film was revealed in the first 10 minutes, why on earth would you want to stay for the rest of the movie? What's to keep your attention, to leave you wanting more?

The same thing applies to dating. Don't give away too much about yourself on your first date. Think verbal striptease tactics. Go slowly, revealing a little at a time rather than putting everything on display all at once. Remaining slightly mysterious is very sexy.

PHONING A FRIEND

Don't even think about picking up the phone. Chatting to your friends when you're on a date is simply ill-mannered. And don't be tempted to send any furtive text messages: if you're caught, your date will think you're bored or gossiping behind their back. Turning your phone off is the considerate thing to do, but if you're really expecting an urgent call, tell your date at the start. At least this shows good manners in forewarning them of a possible interruption.

COMPLAINING ABOUT AGE

When a contributor comes on the show and says, 'I'm 30 years old and feel that time is running out for me. I'm getting old', I get really cross. Telling somebody your age is one thing. Creating an image of yourself sitting in front of a fire, tartan blanket over your knees as you take an afternoon nap is something entirely different. Also, how desperate does it seem? Your date could be excused for thinking you'd prefer to skip dessert in favour of window-shopping for wedding presents. On the other hand, they might equate your attitude with dullness and head for the hills.

It's daft to think of age in negative terms. Being older is a positive attribute: it means you have more experience and more to offer, which is very sexy.

Remember: nervousness is no excuse for bad manners. Treat others with courtesy and consideration and they should do the same for you.

Conclusion

You've read the book, you've done your homework and are now feeling pretty good about yourself? Congratulations! The only thing left to do now, is let The New You loose on the world! But don't misunderstand this term, *Would Like To Meet* isn't about making someone a different person, it's about maximising their potential on all levels – reorganizing what's already there so that the really good bits are obvious and the not-so-fab attributes aren't. Our aim is to reach inside, find that great person buried under a pile of self-doubt and liberate them. Then, as they stand blinking in the sunlight, the trick is to boost their self-esteem sky-high with the right exterior packaging and inner confidence. Add a huge dollop of attitude – knowing what you want and having the conviction and courage to believe you'll get it – and your true self can't help but shine!

Now all that's left to do is push you out of your comfort zone.

Reading this book is the easy part. It's all well and good knowing the theory of what to wear, how to flirt, what to say and how to say it, but it's not going to get you anywhere unless you put it all into practice. Which means (gulp!) walking out of your front door and into the world and (double gulp!) getting out there and approaching people you fancy. There's been a lot of emphasis on this point throughout the book but it's soooooooooo crucial to your dating success, and so we are taking one last opportunity to hit you over the head with it.

Getting people to march right up to sexy strangers provides most of the cringe moments on *WLTM*. You know, the bits that you watch through your fingers and think 'Oh God, no way could I do that'. It's the one task that contributors usually fear the most, but here's the good news – it's also the fear they get over most quickly.

Why is it that talking to strangers makes people feel so anxious? It's most likely because they worry about looking stupid or being completely ignored, or they have a fear of being rejected. Often, it's a tummy-turning combination of all three which accounts for the dry mouth, wobbly knees and pounding heart as you cross the room to meet someone new. How do most contributors feel before we push them off in the right direction? Utterly terrified. How do they feel a few minutes later when they've done the deed and are safely back at our side? Terrific. Beyond terrific, actually. And that's without exception. Would they do it again? Not one contributor hesitated for a moment. In fact, most are so impressed with themselves (and the result) that they're off and at it again within two seconds flat. After that, it's more a case of trying to stop them chatting to strangers so that we can get a word in edgeways and continue doing our jobs.

'Yeah right', I hear you say, 'No way is it that easy'. But actually, it really is that easy. When you've done it once, you've conquered the fear and the next time you do it is much less intimidating. Be brave and don't be afraid to march right over and try it because it rarely, if ever, backfires – even if your target turns out to be married with eight children, a dog, cat and budgie. After all, who isn't going to be secretly chuffed to be complimented on their smile/great outfit/long eyelashes? Just remember if you keep it nice, light, non-threatening and cheerful then you simply can't go wrong. Think about it: it's only a few minutes of feeling uncomfortable in return for a lifetime of chatting easily to whoever you want. Seems like a fair trade to us!

If you were one of our contributors on the show now, this would be the moment when you'd press the buzzer and tell us to 'Buzz off!' (albeit ever so politely). Armed with all the new skills you've learnt from this book, you're now ready, willing and able to go it alone. So at this point we'll do what we do with our in-the-flesh contributors: blow a kiss, wave a fond farewell and hope that you know that we're with you in spirit, every step of the way.

Good luck and thank you for letting us into your lives.

Tracey, Jay and Jeremy

Index

Acknowledgements

This book would not be possible without the outstandingly talented and dedicated Talkback Production Team. Without their constant ideas and enthusiasm, neither the book or television series would have been created. Not only were the creative teams a constant source of ideas and enthusiasm, they became our friends. To say their was a team spirit is the understatement of the millennium.

Many, many thanks to: Daisy Goodwin, Alannah Richardson, Henry Wilks, Simon Bissett, Emma Davis, Jenny Frielich, Mary Paraskakis, Nigel Shilton, Kalita Corrigan, Oscar Challis, Neil Calow, Gavin Searle, Ita Fitzgerald, Kirsty Hanson, Will Parry, Helen Simpson, Debbie Moore, Heidi Bell, Belinda Gregg, Jane Atkinson, Dominic Hill, Anna Paolozzi, Gemma Shanley, Esther Lochrie and Vics Elson. A huge thank you also to our camera and sound crews for giving 150% to the project.

We would also like to thank Cat Ledger, Nicky Copeland, Trish Burgess and Helena Caldon at BBC Books for slaving away and sacrificing glorious long summer nights and weekends to knock this book into shape.

Thank you also to the many reviewers and journalists who gave us the big thumbs-up and to all of you who've written, emailed or phoned to say how much you like the show, and to Nicola Moody, Celia Taylor and Jane Root from the BBC who green-lighted the show

Finally, an enormous and heartfelt thank you to all the contributors from series one and two, who let us into their homes and their hearts and had enough faith to realise all our criticisms and bossing about were for a purpose. It was your honesty and openness that made the programme such a success.

Further reading

The Good Girl's Guide to Bad Girl's Sex, Barbara Keesling,
M Evans & Co Inc, 2001.
Flirt Coach, Peta Heskell, Harper Collins, 2001.
How to Talk to Anyone, Leil Lowndes, Harper Collins, 1999.
How to improve your confidence, Dr Kenneth Hambly,
Sheldon Press, 1987.
Conversationally speaking, Alan Garner, Lowell House, 1997.

Remember – any glossy fashion magazines are good homework for men and women and can provide loads of helpful style tips!

Notes